Recipes

Also by the author

*Ultimate Grandmother Hacks:
50 Kickass Traditional Habits for a Fitter You*

Fix It with Food: Superfoods to Become Super Healthy

The Don't-Diet Plan!: A No-Nonsense Guide to Weight Loss

The Immunity Diet Fight off Infections and Live Your Best Life

500 Recipes

easy, delicious, healthy

SIMPLE TRICKS FOR STRESS-FREE COOKING

KAVITA DEVGAN

RUPA

Published by
Rupa Publications India Pvt. Ltd 2023
7/16, Ansari Road, Daryaganj
New Delhi 110002

Sales centres:
Prayagraj Bengaluru Chennai
Hyderabad Jaipur Kathmandu
Kolkata Mumbai

Copyright © Kavita Devgan 2023

The views and opinions expressed in this book
are the author's own and the facts are as reported by her
which have been verified to the extent possible,
and the publishers are not in any way liable for the same.

All rights reserved.

No part of this publication may be reproduced, transmitted,
or stored in a retrieval system, in any form or by any means,
electronic, mechanical, photocopying, recording or otherwise,
without the prior permission of the publisher.

P-ISBN: 978-93-5702-231-6
E-ISBN: 978-93-5702-237-8

Second impression 2024

10 9 8 7 6 5 4 3 2

The moral right of the author has been asserted.

Printed in India

This book is sold subject to the condition that it shall not, by way of trade
or otherwise, be lent, resold, hired out, or otherwise circulated, without
the publisher's prior consent, in any form of binding or cover other than
that in which it is published.

*To my papa, the most passionate foodie I knew.
Miss you every day.*

Contents

Foreword by Chef Manish Mehrotra — xi
Prologue — xiii

Part 1
Grain Bowls

1. The Ultimate Grain Bowl — 3
2. The Might of Millets — 14
3. A Healthy Barley Twist — 19
4. A Bounty of Rice — 23

Part 2
The Dal Drawer

5. The Versatile Besan — 45
6. The Multifaceted Chickpeas — 48
7. Kickass Kala Chana — 53
8. Lobia: The Hidden Gem — 57
9. Sattu: An Indian Superfood — 60
10. Toor and Moong: Everyday Super Dals — 64

Part 3
Protein Power

11. Eggscellent! — 71
12. Peppy Paneer — 77
13. Fall in Love with Tofu — 82
14. Tiny Fish, Big Benefits — 87

15.	The Dynamite Chicken	90
16.	Chill with Curd	95

Part 4
The Vegetable Rack

17.	The Many Ways to Eat Beetroot	105
18.	Cauliflower Calling	110
19.	Cool as a Cucumber	116
20.	Relishing Bottle Gourd	120
21.	Mushroom Delights	125
22.	Don't Worry, Pea Happy	129
23.	One Potato, Two Potato	133
24.	Pumpkin Is Not Just for Halloween	141
25.	Super Spinach	147
26.	Awesome Zucchini	151
27.	The French Bean Wonder	156
28.	Brilliant Broccoli	158

Part 5
The Fruits Shelf

29.	Banana Treats	163
30.	Summery Raw Mango	168
31.	Delicious Raw Papaya	172
32.	Avocado: the Nutty Taste of Health	177

Part 6
Healthy Sweets

33.	Halwa Happiness	183
34.	Fruits Make Perfect Desserts	185
35.	Delicious Home-Made Laddoos	189
36.	Smart Summer Desserts	192

Part 7
Snack Attack

37.	Power Snacks for Your Workstation	197
38.	Easy-Peasy Chai Snacks	200
39.	Chip-Chip Hooray!	206

Part 8
The Bonus Section

40.	Breakfast for Singles	211
41.	Jazz Up Your Breakfast: Go Regional	214
42.	A Quick Working Lunch	217
43.	Easy, Breezy Dinners for Singles	226
44.	One-Bowl Meals	229
45.	Leftover Delights	233
46.	Reusing Peels and Stems	236
47.	Meals to Make Your Heart Happy	240
48.	Healthy Rainy-Day Recipes	243
49.	Chutney Love	247
50.	In a Pickle!	252

Part 9
Guilt-Free Festival Feasting

51.	The Delicious Grains of Navratri	259
52.	Diwali Ready with Healthy Snacks	263
53.	Gifting Some Home-Made Happiness	265
54.	Healthy and Delicious Festive Sweets	267

Acknowledgements	270

Foreword

As a chef, my job entails working insane hours in the kitchen, endlessly testing recipes, conjuring flavour combinations and giving my (sometimes literal) blood and sweat to my kitchen. And I completely understand that many of us are not keen to spend that kind of time cooking and would much rather order in. I also believe that it takes a person with a particular kind of knowledge to inspire confidence that food can bring joy, and simple, everyday but delicious foods can be cooked in quick and easy ways.

With her relaxed style of writing, cleverly breaking down recipes focussing on a single ingredient, Kavita Devgan invites home cooks back into the kitchen. What is compelling about the book is that Kavita takes an impressive range of recipes and weaves in anecdotes and personal stories from people who have made a mark in various fields. She takes a healthy, light approach to cooking, sharing nutritious yet flavourful recipes that explore the potential of simple ingredients. Her tips for uncommon preparations of common ingredients offer a chance for the reader to experience familiar foods anew.

The book is sure to become an indispensable resource in your kitchen. In her inimitable style, Kavita proves that cooking your comfort food at the end of a hard day can be easy, simple and joyful.

Chef Manish Mehrotra,
Indian Accent, New Delhi

Prologue

At the outset, I would like to mention that this book is unlike other recipe books. I personally find the recipe books available in bookstores pretty to look at but extremely daunting; they are difficult to follow for daily cooking.

This book is easy to read, follow and practise (I know, for sure, that you will cook these recipes). All the recipes here are very quick, easy, familiar, uncomplicated, tasty and economical to make. I have compiled and categorized the recipes (a first, I am told) around one main ingredient. The book does not have pictures, and the recipes are listed in a very easy-to-follow format. It has been formatted like a typical health book while focussing on keeping the recipes accessible and affordable. In a way, this is a health book, a sequel of sorts to my third book, *Fix It with Food: Superfoods to Become Super Healthy*.

The structure of the book, dear readers, allows you to turn to any page and look at the recipes based on the main ingredient of your choice. For instance, if you feel like eating cauliflower, you simply need to open that chapter and choose a recipe. If you want to have a 'fruit only' day, you open the chapters with recipes that only use fruits. Perhaps you only have eggs at home—simply go to the eggs chapter and pick a recipe from there. Maybe your doctor has asked you to begin eating fish—just turn to the seafood section... You get the drift.

I have also included special sections on snacks, desserts, festive fare and a big bonus section with special breakfasts, one-bowl dinners, pickles, chutneys and so much more!

Because the idea behind this book is for you to make these recipes on your own by customizing them as per your preferences, here are a couple of things to keep in mind before you get cooking:

- Most of the recipes in the book serve 1–2 people, but you can adjust the quantities of the ingredients according to the serving you want.
- For baked dishes, adjust the time for and temperature of baking according to your oven's settings.
- Wherever oil has been mentioned, use any oil you prefer.
- Adapt the quantities of spices, nuts, seeds, vegetables according to your personal preferences.

WHO IS THE BOOK MEANT FOR?

This book is meant for anyone who is looking to go back to the basics and cook more at home. It is for anyone trying to eat the way they really should to improve their health and lead a more balanced life.

This book is for all kinds of cooks—those who cook every day, those who step into the kitchen once a week, those who have help at home and even those who usually order in but now want to eat simple, easy-to-make home-cooked fare. This book is for mothers who are tired of planning different menus for all 3 meals (and snacks) day after day, bachelors who want to whip up a quick dinner after work and even people who like to eat a variety of different foods but are not sure how to include vegetables and *dals* (lentils) they have never cooked (or maybe even liked) in their cooking.

A step up from my third book *Fix It with Foods*, this recipe book aims to help people eat all the foods that they know they must include in their diet but don't end up eating for myriad reasons. It also aims to make cooking easy, accessible and fun. It encourages people to cook more at home, which obviously improves their health.

The Covid pandemic and the many infections going around have made everyone realize that it is best to eat more at home, and this lesson is bound to stick. All we need now is the encouragement and self-belief to do it. This book promises to instil these in you.

Along with all this, the book has a couple of amazing anecdotes and food memories from some very special people strewn across the chapters, which make for wonderful reading.

So, it's time to tighten your aprons, and happy cooking, everyone!

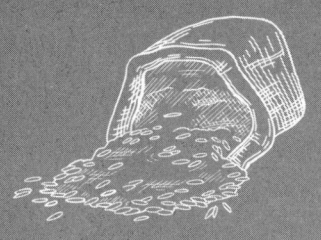

PART 1

Grain Bowls

Even though modern fad diets might say otherwise, it is an irrefutable fact that grains are the mainstay of our meals. And there is a good reason for it. It is almost impossible to meet our nutritional needs if we cut grains out of our diets completely. Grains are so inextricably connected to our food habits that even the dishes we are nostalgic about are, more often than not, made of some grain or the other.

The Benefits of Grains

The benefits of eating grains are immense; some of them have been listed below.

- They keep both our blood sugar levels and moods stable.
- They provide the necessary energy and calories for the smooth functioning of our bodies and their systems.
- They have a lot of gut-strengthening fibre.
- They deliver a multitude of nutrients.
- And, of course, they are, without a doubt, soul-satisfying.

So, eat your carbohydrates but be smart about including them in your diet. You must also remember to always keep rotating your grains, eating as much variety as you can to make the most of the different benefits that each of them delivers.

Who says dishes made with grains have to be basic? You can do a lot more with them than just make roti, puri or dosas. Move beyond just pilaf, rotis, and *khichdi*. Get inventive with grains and plate up one-pot, grain-based salads, soups, desserts and more!

ONE

The Ultimate Grain Bowl

What makes an ultimate grain bowl? Let's begin by discussing the benefits of a variety of grains along with recipes that can be a boon to your health.

DALIYA

Daliya, also known as broken or cracked wheat, is a storehouse of nutrients. It is very rich in fibre, working as a laxative and preventing constipation. It is also a good source of minerals such as iron, calcium, zinc and magnesium, which are very important for heart health. Here are some quick and easy daliya recipes.

Vegetable Daliya

Stir-fry 1 chopped red and yellow pepper each, 50 gm of baby corn with a few cloves of garlic (halved), 1 thickly sliced onion and 5 cashews. Set them aside. Stir-fry 50 gm of daliya, then cook it with some water and set it aside. In a bowl, mix 1 tbsp lemon juice and 1 tbsp olive oil. Add 2 cloves of thinly sliced garlic and a few mint leaves (chopped). Pour this mixture over the vegetables and toss this in with the cooked daliya. Serve hot.

Daliya Dosa

Soak 1 cup of daliya, ½ cup *urad dal* (split black gram), 1 tsp *methi* (fenugreek) seeds in a large bowl for 6 hours. Grind the soaked grains. Leave this batter out to ferment for 8–9 hours. Then, add salt, mix well and use this batter to make thin dosas. Pair with any chutney.

Daliya Mishmash

Mix ½ cup of daliya that has been stir-fried and then cooked in water, ½ cup of boiled chickpeas, 1 cup of steamed and shredded carrots and cabbage and ¼ cup of raw *moong dal* (mung bean) sprouts. Top this up with green chutney or salsa. To increase the protein content, just add a chopped, hard-boiled egg to the bowl.

OATS

Oats are a much-loved breakfast food. They are high in fibre, iron, protein and B vitamins, particularly vitamin B1 (thiamine), which our body needs for carbohydrates to metabolize and for basic cells to function optimally. Oats are a high-satiety food—they make you feel full—so they can be a helpful addition to weight loss plans. Finally, oats contain a specific type of fibre known as beta-glucan, which is known to enhance our immune system and reduce cholesterol. Here are some simple and easy to cook oats recipes.

Apple and Oats Bake

Preheat oven to 177 °C. Lightly oil an 8-inch baking dish. Peel, core and slice 3 apples. Combine them with the juice of ½ a lemon, ¼ tsp ginger paste, ¼ tsp cinnamon and 1 tbsp apple juice concentrate. Pour into the baking dish.

Mix assorted nuts (almond, cashews and walnuts), ½ cup of oats, a pinch of baking soda and 2 tbsp honey. Sprinkle it over the apple mixture. Bake for about 20 to 25 minutes, until the topping is golden brown. Enjoy it warm.

Oats Smoothie

Grind 1 kiwi, ½ cup oats that have been stir-fried then cooked in water, 1 chopped banana and a little bit of milk (of any kind) for 30 seconds. Pour the mixture into glasses and add honey to taste. Garnish with some chopped walnuts and a dash of cinnamon and sip away!

QUINOA

Quinoa has more protein than most other grains. It delivers complete protein (with all essential amino acids). It also contains decent amounts of iron, calcium, vitamin E, magnesium, potassium, zinc, iron, vitamin B_9 (folate) and phosphorous. It also has a lot of antioxidants. Two extremely potent flavonoids found in big amounts in quinoa are quercetin and kaempferol, which have anti-inflammatory, anti-depressant, anti-cancer and antiviral properties. Quinoa is loaded with fibre, which helps relieve constipation and heart diseases by reducing high blood pressure and diabetes. Here are some healthy and quick quinoa recipes.

Orange Saffron Quinoa

Combine ¼ cup of boiled quinoa and ¼ cup of orange juice in a pan and cook over medium heat, stirring constantly till the juice begins to simmer. Then, add 2–3 strands of saffron and cook till the mixture thickens and resembles a halwa. Top with candied almonds or walnuts and serve.

Spinach Broccoli Quinoa Salad

Boil 1 cup of quinoa in 2 cups of water. Place the cooked quinoa in a small pot with broth. Heat until the broth begins to boil. Then, reduce the heat and cover the pot. Simmer for 15 minutes or until the liquid has been completely absorbed.

For the dressing: Mix the juice of ½ a lemon, 1 clove of garlic (minced), 1 tsp ground turmeric, ½ tsp sea salt and ¼ tsp black pepper. Then, whisk in ¼ cup of olive oil.

Assemble the salad: Mix ¼ cup red pepper, ¼ cup green pepper, ¼ cup onion, 1 cup baby spinach (if you have normal spinach [*palak*], blanch it) and 1 cup broccoli. Microwave the mix for 1 minute with 2 tbsp water and then drain it in a large bowl. Add the warm quinoa to the bowl. Pour the dressing over the ingredients and toss to combine. Garnish with 2 tbsp pumpkin seeds. Serve warm or chilled.

Oats and Quinoa Porridge

Lightly roast ¼ cup quinoa and oats each for a few minutes. Add some regular or almond milk and cook on a low flame for about 5 minutes or till the mixture is cooked. Add honey to taste. Garnish with a pinch each of cinnamon and nutmeg, 25 gm chopped mixed nuts and 1 tbsp flaxseeds. Chill before serving.

Quinoa with Shrimp and Beans

Cook 30 gm of quinoa in salted water and keep it aside. Stir-fry or deep-fry 200 gm of shrimp in any oil of your choice and set it aside. Heat 1 tbsp oil in a pan and temper cumin and methi seeds in it. Then, sauté a few chopped cloves of garlic and 1 sliced onion till they are golden. Add steamed and halved French beans and 2 slit green chillies to the pan and cook for 2–3 minutes. Add the shrimp to the pan, along with some salt and spices (red chilli powder and coriander powder). Stir-fry for 2 minutes. Put the cooked shrimp and beans on top of the cooked quinoa, garnish with coriander leaves and dig in!

A Layered Delight

Sauté 1 chopped onion in a pan, crack an egg into it and scramble with a little salt. Cook 30 gm quinoa with a sprinkling of salt. Then, in another bowl, keep 30 gm raw or lightly steamed sprouts seasoned with salt and pepper ready. In a large bowl, layer the cooked quinoa, egg, chopped pineapple or apple and the seasoned sprouts. Sprinkle more salt and pepper, if needed. Dig in!

WHEAT

Paratha

Paratha has been part of our traditional menus for a long time, besides being a part of our Sunday brunch, which makes it a comfort food. However, it is easy to go overboard with paratha, and we can end up consuming more calories and way too much fat when we eat it, thereby undoing the nutritional goodness paratha can deliver.

∽

STORY TIME

Charu Sharma, popularly known as the voice of Indian sports, could not agree more about the goodness of parathas. Charu is an Indian commentator, compere and quizmaster, and director of the famous Pro Kabaddi League. He recalls that while working in his first job in a tea company in Kolkata, he would gorge on unlimited paratha rolls with his bachelor friends. 'They [paratha rolls] used to be very cheap back then, probably a rupee or two each. We would end up eating lots of egg and aloo rolls. I used to have a big appetite in those days, but now it is one-tenth of that,' he recalls. 'But I still love parathas.'

༜

Stuffed parathas can definitely be part of a healthy diet. In fact, they are a perfect way to make some really healthy, otherwise missed ingredients a regular part of our diets. Besides, they are easy to make—just roll out the dough, place the stuffing in the centre, fold the dough, roll flat and cook on the *tawa* on both sides until it's done!

I have listed the top 5 healthy types of paratha stuffing below. Additonally, these types of stuffing make your meal high in protein too!

- Peas (higher in protein than other vegetables)
- Avocado (a good source of heart-healthy monounsaturated fat)
- Lentils (source of protein, fibre and multiple nutrients)
- Beetroot (contains betaine, which helps cleanse the body)
- *Sattu* (provides instant energy and is a source of good quality vegetarian protein)

Now, let me suggest two ways to make parathas smarter, health wise.

- Add a lot of healthy and immunity-boosting spices (garam masala, turmeric, *ajwain* [carom seeds], roasted cumin seeds [*jeera*] and dried ginger) to the stuffing and the dough.
- Don't cook the parathas in too much oil. To make them healthier, add a dollop of ghee on top.

Wrap and Roll!

Wraps and rolls are versatile, convenient, easy-to-carry, non-messy, and the perfect vehicles for multiple different, often-missed-out ingredients. They are also a smart way to combine carbohydrates, fibre and protein in order to ensure maximum health benefits. No wonder then that almost everyone I know loves them so much. It is also the reason why rolls and wraps are a part of every cuisine around the world, including Indian kathi rolls, Mexican burritos, Turkish shawarmas and Vietnamese cold spring rolls.

Here are a few tips to power up your wraps:

- Fortify regular whole wheat flour (*atta*) with extra nutrients by adding 10–20 per cent *besan* (gram flour) or soy flour to it.
- Keep switching the grains in your flour. Eat different grains like whole wheat, amaranth, corn, *ragi* (finger millet), *bajra* (pearl millet) and sattu (roasted gram flour) to get a wider variety of nutrients.
- Get experimental with the types of wraps. Use tacos, pita bread, tortillas, lettuce wraps, etc.
- Always include a lean source of protein, like cooked chicken breast, turkey breast, tofu, canned tuna, egg, legumes or beans.
- Fill your wraps up with vegetables. Eating more vegetables can help you lose weight because they are low in calories and high in fibre; they are also loaded with antioxidants.
- Be creative! Leftovers can be healthy, low-calorie fillings for lunch wraps.
- Keep the wrap size small to keep a check on the number of calories you are consuming.

Here are a few delicious, easy to cook wraps that will change how you cook them.

Avocado Salsa Delight

Heat 1 tsp oil and add 1 sprig of chopped spring onion, thinly sliced, and cook until it is tender. Add ¼ cup of sweet corn and cook through. Then, add ½ avocado, peeled and cut into small pieces. Cook till it softens a bit and season with 1 tsp lime juice, 1 tbsp salsa, salt and pepper.

Place the mixture on a wheat roti, fold it over and secure it with a toothpick. Place the wrap in the same pan and toast until it is lightly browned on both sides. Serve with some salsa on the side.

Corn and Cheese Wrap

Roast 1 medium-sized corn on a direct flame. Set it aside on a plate to cool. Once cooled, cut the kernels out from the cob. Mix 20 gm feta cheese, 20 gm salsa, 1 sprig of chopped spring onion and the roasted corn kernels in a bowl. Place this mixture on a roti, fold the roti over the filling and secure it with a toothpick. Grill the roti wrap in the oven (preheated to 190 °C, turning over for about 1–2 minutes or until it has browned on both sides.

Toss a few torn lettuce leaves with 1 tsp olive oil, ½ tsp vinegar, pepper and salt to taste. Serve the roti wrap with this salad.

Chicken and Sesame Wrap

Marinate 200 gm cubed chicken breast with oregano, salt and freshly ground black pepper to taste. Heat 1 tsp oil in a pan and add the marinated chicken to it. Sauté until the chicken is cooked through. Transfer the chicken to a plate and cover it with foil to keep it warm.

To make the tahini sauce, whisk together 1 tbsp sesame seed paste, a little water, 1 tbsp curd, 1 tsp lemon juice and 1 crushed garlic clove in a bowl. Add a pinch of chilli flakes, salt and pepper to taste.

Take a roti, place a few torn lettuce leaves, a few slices of cucumber and tomato, the cooked chicken mix and 1 sliced sprig of spring onion on it. Drizzle some tahini sauce on top. Wrap the roti around the filling. Serve with mustard sauce.

Beetroot Salad Roll

Wrap 150 gm beetroot in aluminium foil and roast in an oven for about 1 hour at 200 °C until it is tender. Remove from the oven and allow it to cool. Slice the roasted beetroot into thin rounds. Place the beetroot in a bowl and top it with 100 gm cherry tomatoes sliced in half. Garnish with 50 gm of crumbled feta cheese and a few mint leaves. Season with salt and pepper to taste. Place the mixture on a roti, roll and serve. (Note: Roasted beetroots can stay in the fridge for a week to be used again.)

Vegan Lettuce Roll

To make the sauce, whisk together 1 tbsp tamari (gluten-free soy sauce), 1 tbsp maple syrup, ½ tbsp vinegar, ½ tsp each of ginger and garlic pastes.

For the stuffing, heat 1 tbsp olive oil in a pan, add a julienned carrot, ½ yellow capsicum and 1 sprig of spring onion. Add the sauce we made earlier, simmer and cook for about 10–15 minutes.

Take the mixture off the heat. Toss ½ tbsp each of halved dry roasted peanuts and cashews into it. Let the mixture cool and then scoop it into two large lettuce leaves. Garnish with salt and red pepper flakes, roll it up and dig in.

5 Really Quick Rolls

- **Sweet Delight:** Mix shredded apple, shredded cheddar and maple syrup. Put the mixture in the oven for a minute at 200 °C to melt the cheese before wrapping it up in a roti roll.
- **Bean-y Delight:** Mix leftover cooked rice and baked beans. Season with salt and pepper flakes. Garnish with a little shredded cheese. Roll this up in a roti, paratha or tortilla.
- **Egg Delight:** Sauté some onion and red pepper. Scramble 2 eggs into this mixture. Garnish with a cheese of your choice. Roll this stuffing up in a roti, paratha or tortilla.
- **Fruity Delight:** Spread some peanut or almond butter on a roti. Place a chopped banana and strawberries on top. Drizzle some maple syrup, roll it up and dig in.
- **Vegetable Delight:** Spread cream cheese on a warm tortilla. Place your favourite vegetables, like shredded and steamed carrot, zucchini, spinach, broccoli, raw cucumber and tomatoes in it. Season with salt, pepper and herbs, roll it up and serve.

COUSCOUS

Couscous is a good source of fibre that prevents blood sugar spikes and keeps you fuller for longer. It also contains the rare, immune-supportive mineral selenium. Couscous is also extremely versatile and helps add variety to our diet.

Pumpkin, Couscous and Chickpeas Salad

Stir-fry ½ cup of couscous then cook it in water. Let it sit for 5–6 minutes before fluffing it gently with a fork. Mix the cooked couscous with ½ cup of roasted pumpkin, ¼ cup of rocket leaves, ½ cup of boiled chickpeas and 3–4 toasted walnuts.

For the dressing, whisk 1 tbsp olive oil, salt to taste, ½ tsp paprika and 1 tsp lemon juice together. Pour it over the couscous mix and serve.

BUCKWHEAT

Buckwheat (*kuttu*) is loaded with B vitamins and high-quality protein. It also contains lysine, an essential amino acid that is usually missing from most of our staple grains, like wheat and rice. Lysine is known to help absorb more calcium from our diet. This is a big plus, especially for vegetarians. Buckwheat is loaded with fibre, too, which helps keep hunger pangs at bay and cravings in check.

Buckwheat Noodle Bowl

Boil 100 gm buckwheat noodles in salted water and set them aside. In a heated pan, add 1 tsp olive oil and ½ cup sprouts. Stir-fry for a few minutes. Then, add ½ cup sliced mushrooms, 100 gm spinach and cook with a cup of water. Then, add 1 tsp soy sauce, 1 tbsp sliced ginger, 2 cloves of sliced garlic, 1 tsp vinegar and 1 tsp honey or maple syrup. Add the noodles to the pan and sauté. Garnish with 1 tsp sesame seeds and ¼ of a thinly-sliced red bell pepper.

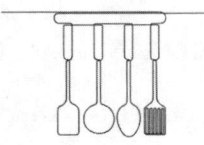

TWO

The Might of Millets

What's old is new again. Suddenly, all sorts of whole grains are being embraced by home cooks and restaurants. They are more widely available in supermarkets as well. Leading the pack are the mighty millets.

Why does this make me so happy? Well, it's because I have always believed that millets definitely deserve a spot on your plate. Rich in fibre, protein, B vitamins and other nutrients, these ancient grains are extremely versatile and can be swapped for pasta or rice in dishes, added to salads and power bowls and even prepared like oatmeal for a warm breakfast bowl topped with fruits and nuts. Another bonus for environmentally conscious people is that millets require little water and grow well in arid and semi-arid regions of the world. Thus, consuming millets has a lower carbon footprint than other foods. This could be your contribution to ensuring that we leave behind some food for the future generations.

THE BENEFITS OF MILLETS

The dense, earthy flavour of millets is an acquired taste, especially because our palate has become used to the relative blandness of wheat and white rice. However, eating millets is immensely beneficial. I have listed some benefits below.

- Millets are gluten-free grains. So, they are a boon for those who are gluten intolerant and even for those who generally wish to reduce the gluten in their diet.
- It is now a well-proven fact that consuming millets regularly can help you lose weight due to the high levels of fibre and bioactive compounds in them.
- Millets are also rich in fibre, protein, B vitamins and other nutrients. Thus, they are extremely versatile.

BOOST MILLETS' SUPERPOWER: SPROUT THEM

To make the most of millets, sprout them before consumption. Sprouts have been a buzzword for healthy eating for a long time now. But, somehow, they have become synonymous with sprouted dals, like moong, *chana* (split chickpea or Bengal gram) and *lobia* (black-eyed peas). And even though such sprouts have been around for a while, they haven't really become mainstream yet. Let's change that!

Why Eat Sprouts?

Sprouting increases the nutritional value of all grains by leaps and bounds, boosting the content of B and C vitamins, minerals, antioxidants and other key nutrients. It also makes these nutrients more bioaccessible (more easily absorbable by the body). This is extremely helpful in the case of iron, in particular, a mineral that is difficult to absorb from vegetarian sources.

Sprouted grains also have a lower glycaemic index (GI), which is an indicator of how quickly and how high a particular food raises blood sugar levels, and are easily digestible due to the enzyme activity that peaks during the process. On sprouting, the starchy carbohydrates in the seed get converted to energy. So, the resulting sprouted grain has a higher ratio of protein and fibre to carbohydrates.

Proteins also become more digestible when the grain is sprouted. The biggest benefit is that sprouting helps decrease the presence of anti-nutrients (like phytic acid, enzyme inhibitors, lectins, saponins, etc.), which are the naturally occurring compounds found in plant seeds that interfere with our ability to digest vitamins and minerals in the plants.

Sprouting Ideas

Sprouted grains can be eaten raw, lightly cooked, ground into flour or turned into bread. So, toss a handful of sprouted grains in a salad, stir-fry or soup, or simmer them in milk to make porridge. I remember eating home-made sprouted ragi bread at a homestay in Uttarakhand a long time ago. I am sure it did my body a lot of good, and the taste…it still remains with me.

CHANGE HOW YOU COOK MILLETS

Here are a few delicious millet recipes that are also easy to cook.

Ragi

This underrated gluten-free grain has a lot going for it. It is a rich source of calcium and iron and its main protein fraction, eleusine has a high biological value, which means it is easily absorbed and used in the body. It is also a very rich source of minerals. It has much more calcium content compared to other cereals.

Ragi Kuzhu (Porridge)

Add 30 gm ragi powder to normal water, mix it well and then boil it. Mixing it before boiling will avoid forming lumps. Keep boiling the mixture until it reaches a viscous consistency.

Add salt to taste, stir and take it off the flame. Squeeze the juice of 1 lemon and salt to 250 ml buttermilk (*chaach*). Pour the buttermilk mixture into the cooked ragi. Serve with lime pickle. You can even cook the ragi at night, leave it in the fridge overnight and simply add buttermilk in the morning before digging in.

Ragi Soup

Mix 2 tbsp ragi flour with water to make a paste. In a pan, add a pinch of cumin, ½ a chopped onion, ½ a chopped carrot, a few chopped beans and 1 tbsp peas. Cook with a little water till the vegetables are done. Then, add the ragi paste, salt and pepper to taste, 1 tbsp cream or 2 tbsp coconut milk and some water (until the mixture reaches a soupy consistency) and simmer for 5 minutes while stirring constantly. Squeeze some lemon juice and garnish with chopped cashews before digging in.

Bajra

Bajra is a brilliant detoxing agent. It also contains catechins, like quercetin, which help keep the kidney and liver functioning properly by excreting toxins from the body.

Bajra Pongal

Dry roast ¾ cup of broken bajra till it is mildly heated. Pressure cook the roasted broken bajra with ¼ cup of green gram dal (keep the bajra and dal ratio to 70:30) and salt to taste in 3 cups of water for 3 whistles on low heat, until it is soft. Heat some ghee and shallow-fry a few cashews in it until they are slightly golden brown. Then, add cumin seeds, pepper, curry leaves and ginger paste to the heated oil before pouring it over the pongal. Have it with buttermilk.

Bajra Khichdi

Grind ½ cup of bajra coarsely in a grinder and mix it with an equal amount of moong dal. Transfer the mixture to a pressure cooker with 2 cups of water and salt. Cook for 3 whistles on low heat. Add a *tadka* (tempered spices) made in ghee with mustard seeds, curry leaves, dried red chillies on top along with 2 sliced deseeded green chillies.

Jowar (Sorghum)

Jowar is loaded with nutrients. While the calcium content in jowar is similar to wheat and rice, it contains a good amount of iron, protein and fibre. It is also rich in policosanols, which help reduce bad cholesterol.

Jowar Khichdi

Soak jowar in water for a few hours. Cook for 1 whistle on high flame and then on low flame for 15 minutes. Heat some oil, add ½ tsp cumin seeds, a few curry leaves, 1 tsp ginger garlic paste, a cubed and boiled potato and few other vegetables. Add the cooked jowar along with roasted crushed peanuts, salt to taste and 1 tsp sugar. Mix well, squeeze some lemon juice on top and serve.

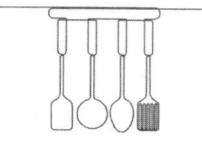

THREE

A Healthy Barley Twist

Grain rotation is the perfect way to ensure a more balanced intake of nutrients. Including barley (*jau*) regularly in your diet is a good step towards grain rotation. It helps keep your blood sugar in check too.

BENEFITS OF BARLEY

Some of the immense benefits of eating barley have been listed below.

- This grain has a lower GI and helps control the rise of blood sugar levels.
- It is rich in soluble fibre, which can form a gel when mixed with liquids in the stomach. This slows down the emptying of the stomach, which prevents carbohydrates from being absorbed too quickly and keeps a check on rising blood sugar levels.
- It is a rare vegetarian grain source of complete protein— it has all 8 essential amino acids and is loaded with manganese, selenium, phosphorus, copper, magnesium, iron, zinc, potassium and some calcium too.

CHANGE HOW YOU COOK BARLEY

You can, of course, make barley rotis, but here are a few delicious barley recipes that are also easy to cook.

Home-Made Sports Drink

Rinse 1 cup of pearl barley under cold water a few times. Then, place it in a pan with 1 tbsp lemon peel and 2 cups of water. Bring it to a boil; then, simmer for 15–30 minutes. Strain the mixture into a bowl. Keep the barley aside and use it to make another dish. Stir in some honey and the juice of 2 lemons to the strained barley water. Let the mixture cool down to room temperature. Chill and drink.

Barley Stir-fry

Stir-fry some mixed (red, yellow, green) peppers, 100 gm boiled chicken pieces and lots of garlic in 1 tbsp of oil. Add 1 cup of boiled barley pearls to the mixture. Toss in 2 tbsp peri peri sauce before serving.

For peri peri sauce, blitz ½ a red pepper, 2 dried red chillies, some garlic, a few mint leaves, 1 tbsp vinegar, 1 tbsp oil, salt and pepper to taste.

Barley Delight

Cook 1 cup of pearl barley with 200 gm grated vegetables (carrot, baby corn, mushrooms) and set aside on a plate. Top it off with 50 gm of grated cheese and a pan-fried egg seasoned with salt and pepper.

Cold Barley Salad

Boil 1 cup of pearl barley, strain and set aside. Sauté 1 red and yellow bell pepper each, 100 gm mushrooms, 50 gm baby corn and 50 gm French beans. Mix them with the barley, add chopped coriander and 2 sliced boiled eggs. Season with salt, pepper, oregano and red chilli flakes. Chill the salad before serving.

Baked Barley with Vegetables and Cheese

Soak 1 cup of barley for 2 hours. Pressure cook in vegetable stock or water with 1 cup of chopped assorted cubed vegetables, a few garlic flakes and salt and pepper to taste. Cook for 2 whistles on high flame and 10 minutes on low flame. Transfer to a baking tray and let it cool. Grate some cheese on top, put it in a preheated to 200 °C oven for 10 minutes before serving.

Barley, 2 Ways

- For a wholesome breakfast, soak a big batch of barley for 2 hours. Boil it in water. Toss in walnuts, honey and a dash of cinnamon.
- Next day, for lunch, make a savoury barley preparation. Season the boiled barley with salt, pepper and herbs of your choice. Top it off with a fried egg and a sauce of your choice.

Barley Roll

Cook 1 cup of soaked barley for 20–30 minutes or until it is cooked through. Let it cool. Roll it up in plastic wrap. Chill for a few hours. Unwrap and slice. Grill or sauté the barley slices. Top the barley slices with 200 gm of grilled meat or fish, 1 cup of assorted roasted vegetables and 2 tbsp salsa.

Mutton Barley

Cook 200 gm boneless mutton in a little oil over medium-high flame for 3–4 minutes or until it has browned. Remove the mutton from the pan and set it aside. In the same pan, add

1 cup of mixed chopped vegetables (carrots, potatoes, onion and mushrooms). Place a lid on the pan and let the vegetables cook until they are tender. Add ¼ cup of tomato purée and cook for a couple more minutes. Transfer the browned mutton and the cooked vegetables to a pressure cooker with barley that has been pre-soaked for a few hours. Add some water, spices of your choice and salt. Let the water start boiling over high heat. Close the lid of the cooker and cook for 2 whistles on high heat and then on sim for 20–25 minutes. Pair with a raita.

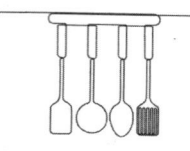

FOUR

A Bounty of Rice

How many good foods can you stop eating just because some half-baked news reports say they are bad for us? Rice, particularly white rice, is a clear case in point. It has been maligned lately by self-appointed health food faddists. Don't listen to the naysayers! Rice is actually quite good for your heart.

I have grown up eating rice. In fact, most of the meals my mom served ended with rice. She would always say that eating rice is a symbol of prosperity and happiness. I would go a step further and say that eating rice also makes us healthy! Along with it, rice is actually extremely flexible—it can be cooked as an entrée, a main or a dessert!

Ask anyone what food they turn to for comfort and chances are most of them will mention rice. *Dal bhaat, meethe chawal*, curd rice, lemon rice and myriad other rice-based dishes will be mentioned, all with umpteen stories and memories attached. I remember *gud chawal* being an important part of my growing up years. My mother would make it for us before and after exams, on birthdays and whenever my sister or I would crave something sweet. This dish was my mother's way of feeding us a quick, home-made, wholesome dessert, one she knew was good for us.

BENEFITS OF RICE

Everyone needs a certain number of calories daily for their bodies to function. Whatever the latest fad diet or weight loss bestseller might say, going off carbohydrates in an effort to lose weight is a big NO. Doing that might just wreak havoc on your hormones. So, skip the guilt and enjoy rice in the right portions.

I am not trying to give rice a clean chit—no food deserves or gets that, but it is definitely not the villain it is being made out to be. The benefits of eating rice are immense. I have listed some of them below.

- Rice is a good source of healthy carbohydrates that provide the much-needed energy to get us through the day.
- Rice is a perfect food, piggybacking on which we can consume a lot of fibre and protein. Case in point: vegetable dal khichdi, chicken biryani, soy rice and so on.
- Rice eaters, in fact, tend to have better diet quality and nutrient intake.

For me, the criticism that white rice has a higher GI does not hold water. This is because rice is rarely eaten alone, and its pairing with other foods reduces its GI by slowing down its digestion.

Rice is eaten across our country, probably for almost every meal in the southern and northeastern states. Similarly, the Japanese eat at least 1 rice-based dish per day. In fact, they believe it is rude to leave any rice in their bowls. And despite this, as we all know, the rate of obesity is the lowest in Japan. I was in the country a couple of years ago and I ate the short-grain sticky rice for most of my meals during my 5 days there. We can compare that to cultures that don't eat rice at all. Besides, as with any other food, portion size is obviously important.

There are as many varieties of rice in India as there are dialects, with each region producing a variety. White rice, too, is okay to eat every now and then because, no, it is not a sugar-spiking villain if it is had with dals and vegetables. However, it is a good idea to eat the many indigenous rice varieties we grow in the country too, as they are extremely beneficial for us.

∽

STORY TIME

Chitra Narayanan, a journalist, author and a hobby cook, has a point to make here. According to her, it's amazing how, as you grow older, you find comfort in the food you grew up with. One of her favourite breakfast foods these days is *upma kozhukattai*—a dish that her mom often used to make at home and which she confesses was not among her favourites as a kid. But now, she has begun appreciating this healthy and flavourful dish, which can be dressed up with sumptuous accompaniments like a brinjal *gotsu* (a traditional South Indian gravy made with brinjal and moong dal) on a weekend or had with just a chutney on busy weekdays.

According to her, what *modak* is to Maharashtrians, kozhukattai is to Tamilians. However, she adds that today, the festive kozhukattai that used to be offered as divine *prasad* to Lord Ganesha has been adapted into a breakfast or an evening tiffin item by enterprising souls and the recipe has made its way into most Tamilian households.

The traditional kozhukattai involves making a rice dough, rolling it out and then stuffing it with a mix of jaggery and coconut for the sweet version or a spicy filling of urad dal for a savoury version. The latter is delicious but cumbersome to make, as the urad dal has to be soaked for several hours, ground with ginger and red chillies, and then cooked with coconut.

The upma kozhukattai, on the other hand, is a shortcut version that is also highly adaptable—you can use your imagination and substitute rice with oatmeal, millets or even prepare versions with dals to make it even more healthy or for variety.

Chitra's Upma Kozhukattai: Rice Dumplings, Tamil Nadu Style!

In a pan, heat 1 tbsp oil and temper some red chillies, mustard seeds, urad dal, curry leaves and *hing* (asafoetida) in it till it all splutters. Soak 2 tbsp moong dal for 15 minutes. To it, add 2 tbsp grated carrot and 2 tbsp grated coconut and mix well. Add 2.5 cups of water and let it come to a boil. Then, stir in a bit of salt to taste. Now take 1 cup of rice flour (you can either use ready-made flour or soak a cup of rice for 30 minutes, dry it on a cloth and then grind it) and add it bit by bit to the boiling water, stirring all the while, until it solidifies to the consistency of upma. Switch the gas off and let the upma rest.

While the upma cools, prepare *arachakalaki* chutney. In a mixer, blend $\frac{1}{2}$ cup of grated fresh coconut, 1 gooseberry, 1 tbsp curd and salt and green chillies to taste. Add some water until the blended mixture reaches the consistency of a runny chutney. Garnish with a tadka of mustard seeds and curry leaves made in ghee.

Once the upma has cooled, shape it into oval balls and steam them for 12 to 15 minutes. You can use an idli steamer or even a vessel placed in a pressure pan filled with water (without the weight) to steam the upma balls.

Serve hot with arachakalaki chutney. It can be paired with *sambar* or *gotsu* too.

Note: To make the kozhukattai even healthier, you could add oats, millet ragi powder or powdered dals to the rice powder mix—make a multigrain kozhukattai, so to speak.

∽

POHA

Poha (flattened rice) is a favourite ingredient across the country, and many people are introduced to it during their travels. It is prepared and eaten in multiple ways. It is an easily digestible food, and everyone from infants to elderly people can have it.

∽

STORY TIME

Tarun Sibal, a chef and entrepreneur, said that he had never had poha growing up until his first trip to Mumbai in the fifth grade. 'I remember all of us cousins went with our grandfather to Mumbai during the summer holidays. We used to have a flat and a car there and that's when I got hooked on to poha. Before that, a special Sunday breakfast would be a bread pakora, bread roll, burger or a paratha; poha had been alien to me. After this trip, though, poha became a part of our breakfast repertoire. But my mother had her own recipe. She would make it Punjabi style—no mustard seeds and curry leaves. Instead, our poha would have lots of peas and onions, always with some *bhujia* on top and sometimes peanuts too. It was her version, and I grew up loving it. In fact, it's a given till date that if I feel like having something special, poha is made for me at home. Poha is a fond memory that I have of my first time as a child in Mumbai that I will never forget, and it has gone on to become a food habit,' shares Sibal.

∽

Poha is supremely healthy. It delivers some iron, which is much needed in these times of rampant iron deficiency and falling haemoglobin levels, along with some B vitamins, particularly vitamin B1, which is essential to properly breakdown carbohydrates and fats.

It is also an energy-laden ingredient that delivers a decent amount of fibre. Furthermore, it is a comfort food that is gluten-free, which helps your digestive system rest.

Change How You Cook Poha

I love the traditional poha recipe with lots of mustard seeds, curry leaves, peanuts, potatoes, peas and a generous squeeze of lemon juice on top, but you could try its variations too.

Now, we all know that the best meals are those that deliver both protein and carbohydrates along with some good fats. So, how can we make poha a perfect carbohydrate- as well as protein-rich dish? Here are a few delicious poha recipes that strike the balance and are also easy to cook.

Tofu and Poha

Take a bowl of cooked poha. Add salt and pepper to taste. In a pan, heat some sesame oil and stir-fry 2 cloves of finely chopped garlic, 1 sliced onion and 2 chopped green chillies. Add chopped tofu pieces and season with salt, chilli sauce, soy sauce and any spicy tomato sauce. Mix well and cook for a few minutes. Mix the tofu with the poha and dig in.

Poha and Masala Moong

Make poha the traditional way and set it aside. Heat oil in a pan and add cumin seeds, hing, sliced onion, green chillies, red chillies, coriander powder, turmeric and salt. Cook for some time. Add boiled green moong dal (or sprouts), sprinkle some water on it and let it cook for 5–8 minutes with a lid on. Garnish with some *amchoor* (dried mango powder). Serve the poha on half the plate and green moong on the other half. Separate them with some curd in between and dig in!

Protein-Rich Poha and Sattu, 2 Ways

- Soak 1 cup of poha in a little water for 5 minutes. Add 1 finely chopped onion, 2 green chillies and some turmeric. Season with salt, black pepper and *chaat masala*. Add some crushed roasted peanuts and 1 tbsp of sattu. Mix well. Sprinkle some water to make it a little moist.
- In a pan, dry roast 1 cup of poha for 4–5 minutes and set it aside to cool. Meanwhile, heat oil in a pan, temper a pinch of mustard seeds, hing, curry leaves, peanuts, and urad or chana dal for 1 minute on a low flame. Add turmeric powder, red chilli powder, salt and a pinch of sugar. Then, immediately add the roasted poha and mix well. Take the dish off the heat, add 1 tbsp sattu and mix well before serving.

Eggy Poha

Make poha the traditional way. Then, add sliced, hard-boiled eggs to it. Though a little unique, it is delicious and adds the goodness of egg (which is a complete protein with multiple nutrients) to the dish. If you are a vegetarian, replace egg with soy nuggets boiled in salted water.

Dahi Chura (Curd Poha)

Wash, rinse and drain the poha (chura). Add curd and grated jaggery. Mix well and it's ready to eat. You can also add some nuts for more protein.

You can also make *doodh cheere*, which is rice flakes soaked in milk with chopped bananas (a traditional, favourite breakfast in Bengal).

Maharastrian Gopalkala

Cook ½ cup of poha the traditional way mentioned earlier in the chapter (see p. 28). Mix it with ½ cup curd, ¼ cup pomegranate and ½ a cucumber. This dish is a prasad recipe that is often made on Krishna Janmashtami in Maharashtra.

LEFTOVER RICE

Every household, no matter how hard they try to cook in a limited quantity, ends up with some leftover rice. I feel that's actually a reason to rejoice. One of my all-time favourite comfort dishes is masala curd rice. In fact, I always make some extra rice and leave it overnight in the fridge. Then, the next day I take the rice, mix it with fresh curd, chopped onions, green chillies and sometimes some steamed vegetables too. I top this off with a tadka made in ghee with mustard seeds, hing, dried red chillies and lots of curry leaves before digging in. All is well with the world and my stomach on that day. There is just a lot that you can do with a bowl of leftover rice.

The fact is that boiling rice and keeping it in the fridge to use it the next day does not make it stale. Rather, it surprisingly boosts its health quotient. Had this way, the resistant starch (RS) content of white rice increases tremendously.

Note: RS is a lesser-known type of fibre that our food provides. It is a special kind of starch that passes through the small intestines undigested and unchanged. So, it helps us stay lean and healthy, as it satisfies us, thus helping reduce food intake and fat accumulation.

༄

STORY TIME

Subha J. Rao—a Mangaluru-based journalist and founder of Made in Mangalore by Subha (madeinmangalore.in), a range of home-roasted, home-ground artisanal spice mixes—agrees with me on leftover rice.

She shares that for the most part of their 24-year marriage, her husband Mahesh, a banker, has lived in another city. He's a dal, rice and potato fry kind of guy—that's the 1 meal he has cooked repeatedly and perfected over the years. But, there's one more thing he does fabulously well—embellish the regular *paruppu podi* (dal powder rice) with some minor artistic flourishes.

'Finely chopped onion and curry leaves go into the tadka as do mustard seeds and hing. And then, the day-old refrigerated rice is tossed into the *kadai* along with some dal powder [a happy mix of powdered roasted *toor* (split pigeon peas) dal and chana along with hing and chillies that you can make at home or buy from stores]. He then garnishes it with some finely chopped coriander. It makes for a perfect meal with raita and papad,' she shared.

Subha personally loves to make a mushy pongal with leftover rice. 'Just roast some yellow moong, and cook it along with the rice in a cooker. Temper chopped ginger, cashews, curry leaves and hing in ghee and drizzle it on top along with some cumin-pepper powder and salt. Stir in a ladle of milk for creaminess. Trust me, this tastes much better than pongal made with fresh rice,' she said.

∞

Change How You Cook with Leftover Rice

Every region of the country has a couple of traditional dishes made with leftover rice. There are, in fact, as many ways to cook leftover rice in India as there are cuisines.

We have an array of delectable rice dishes, such as lemon rice, tamarind rice, coconut rice, fried ghee rice and so on. And have you ever tried making a rice patty from leftover rice? It's delicious! Finally, there is an amazing tangy rice recipe that my mother makes with raw mangoes, red chillies and coconut. It's spicy and perfect with raita. I wait every year for the mango season to begin for this dish.

You can even just mix leftover rice with some sattu, salt to taste, dried coconut flakes, finely chopped onions and green chillies, a bit of mustard oil and dry roasted cashews and peanuts.

Note: Boiled and cooled potatoes deliver the same RS benefit too! So, indulge in them and it'll do your gut and health a lot of good. You might even knock off a few pounds without trying.

Here are a few delicious recipes with leftover rice that are also easy to cook.

Maharashtrian Masala Bhaat

In a little coconut oil, temper some mustard seeds and curry leaves. Stir-fry the leftover rice in this. Garnish with roasted peanuts and shredded fresh or dry coconut.

Maharashtrian Phodnicha Bhaat

This is a Maharashtrian version of lemon rice that is prepared mostly for breakfast using leftover rice.

To make it, add mustard and cumin seeds to some hot oil. Then, add chopped green chillies and curry leaves to it. Sauté a chopped onion in the oil with some salt till it's translucent. Add turmeric powder and red chilli powder. Stir in the leftover rice and let it get heated for about 2–3 minutes. Turn off the stove, add a pinch of sugar and squeeze some lemon juice over the rice. Mix well before serving.

Maharashtrian Vangi Bhaat

Take ¾ cup of leftover rice. Dry roast and grind ½ tsp urad dal, 7–8 curry leaves, 1 dry red chilli and 2 tbsp peanuts or 6–7 cashew nuts. Grind the roasted ingredients when they have cooled down and set them aside.

Cut 1 cup of cubed brinjal lengthwise in ½ inch chunks, sprinkle a little turmeric on the pieces. Heat 2 tbsp oil in a thick bottomed pan and fry the cut brinjal.

Add the powdered masala and salt to taste. Remove from the flame and mix in the cooked rice. Add ghee and 1 tbsp lemon juice on top before serving.

(A similar dish is made in Karnataka with tamarind pulp.)

Odia Pakhala Bhaat

This dish is called *panta bhaat* in West Bengal and *poita bhaat* in Assam.

To make it, add water to 1 cup of cooked rice, cover it and leave it to ferment overnight (keep the dish covered to avoid contamination). Next morning, to the soaked rice, add half a chopped onion, 2 chopped green chillies, salt to taste, the juice of half a lemon and perhaps a little roasted brinjal or mashed potato (other additions can be achaar, fried fish, various boiled vegetables, leftover dals or curries from the previous night, etc.). You can even have a little sour curd on the side.

Tamil Pazhedhu Saadham (Old Rice)

This dish is usually made in rural Tamil Nadu. To make it, soak rice in water overnight to prevent spoilage. The next day, mash the soaked rice with buttermilk and salt to make a gruel and serve.

Kerala Style Leftover Rice

Soak leftover rice in water overnight. In the morning, just add green chillies, cooked tapioca, any leftover vegetables, some curd and salt to it. Then, mix it well and enjoy!

KHICHDI

Khichdi derives its name from the Sanskrit word *khicca* and is the original one-pot dish that is complete in itself! I feel it is one of the first masterstrokes of eating healthy the right way. Whoever first thought of it was an absolute genius!

I love khichdi because it gets ready as quickly as most convenience store foods (packaged or ready to eat). You just have to dump the ingredients (dal, rice, vegetables and seasonings) together, cook and 15 minutes later, you can dig in. But the difference is that khichdi is extremely healthy. What's more? Just about everyone has a memory attached to it.

STORY TIME

For **Stutee Ghosh**, a film critic and radio jockey, one strong memory associated with her baba is of *bhog khichdi*. 'Khichdi is usually thought to be food for days when you are sick but bhog khichdi is the stuff of gods! When khichdi is made in Bengali households, it usually comes with accompaniments like *bhaja*—which are fries made from potato, brinjal or pumpkin—*tamatar ki chutney* and papad. The *Bhog* khichdi served during Durga Puja is unmatched in taste and experience. I'm sure people have gone to Puja pandals, which generally serve bhog khichdi that tastes incomparably divine. No matter how well you make *kada prashad* at home, it's never like what you get in a gurdwara. It's the same thing with bhog khichdi,' she shared.

'Baba worked very closely with the Probashi Bengali community here in Delhi. He was a trustee and an active Puja committee member. So, having bhog khichdi with dad and mum at our neighbourhood Puja pandal is a memory I will forever cherish,' she added.

∞

Kiran Manral, a celebrated author, said she became a latchkey kid when she was 9, after her father passed away. 'Mom started working then and had to go off to work at a bank, which was a long distance away. I returned home around 2 after school. I was not allowed to turn on the cooking gas and light it when no one else was at home. So, I would eat my lunch directly from the refrigerator,' she recalled. When Kiran's mom was in a rush in the mornings, her go-to two-minute meal was khichdi. Kiran would eat the plain yellow dal and rice khichdi with Bedekar's mango pickle. 'I ate it directly from the refrigerator—it used to be a congealed hard mess by then. But I think hunger is a great appetite builder, and I used to eat it with relish back then. Cold khichdi to date remains my comfort food—a spoonful and I go back straight to my childhood,' she adds.

∞

Khichdi is a calorie balanced meal that is low in fat, high in fibre, loaded with multiple vitamins and minerals. It also delivers a decent amount of good quality protein in an easily digestible form. In fact, while most vegetarian foods tend to be incomplete sources of protein, this dal chawal combination delivers complete protein (with all essential amino acids). And, as it soaks up water during preparation, it is a hydrating food too. In addition, khichdi raises serotonin levels in the brain, which has a calming, soothing effect on us.

Change How You Cook Khichdi

Khichdi is possibly the most versatile dish ever. Every kitchen has its own special way of making it (yes, somehow it tastes different in every household). There are regional specialities, of course: in Bihar, cauliflower and green peas are often added to it; and a friend tells me that in Maharashtra, it is made with prawns. There's, in fact, a khichdi for everyone. You just have to find one that matches your palate. Here are a few delicious khichdi recipes that are also easy to cook.

The Lazy Khichdi

Soak ½ cup prewashed moong dal and ½ cup rice for at least ½ an hour.

Heat 1 tsp ghee, add a pinch of cumin seeds, hing and 1 tsp grated ginger and a few chopped cloves of garlic. Then, throw in some raw peanuts. Sauté for half a minute. Add the drained rice and dal, along with a pinch of turmeric powder and salt to taste. Sauté for a minute. Add water till the rice mixture is immersed and cook till it's done (between 12–15 minutes). Garnish with fried cashews, thin onion rings and dig in!

Chana Dal Khichdi

Soak 250 gm rice in water for 30 minutes. In 1 tsp heated oil, sauté ½ tsp cumin seeds and 50 gm soaked and drained chana dal for 5 minutes. Then, add 500 ml water and bring to a boil. Add the drained rice. Cover and cook for about 7–8 minutes till it's done.

Coconut Khichdi

Heat 1 tbsp coconut oil, add a pinch each of mustard and cumin seeds, 2 dry red chillies and a few curry leaves. Then, add 1 sliced onion and a few chopped cloves of garlic. Next, add 1 chopped potato, 100 gm chopped pumpkin and 50 gm peas. Stir-fry for 5 minutes. Add salt to taste, ½ tsp garam masala and ½ tsp jaggery. Then, add the drained dal and rice with 200 ml coconut milk and 250 ml water. Mix it up and cook for 3 whistles in a pressure cooker. Garnish with roasted cumin powder and dig in.

Prawn Khichdi

Sauté 1 finely chopped onion and 2 tbsp grated coconut (fresh or dry) for about 7 minutes, till the onions turn a little brown. Cool the mixture and grind it to make a fine paste. Mix 1 cup of washed rice with this paste, add the juice of 1 lemon, 1 tbsp ginger and garlic paste, ½ an inch of sliced ginger and keep this aside for ½ an hour. Meanwhile, marinate 250 gm prawns with some red chilli powder, turmeric and 2 tbsp spicy salsa for an hour and then sauté them for a few minutes. Heat 2 tbsp coconut oil, add 2 cloves, ½ tsp ground cinnamon and 1 finely chopped onion. Add the marinated rice and stir for 2 minutes on low flame. Then, add the marinated prawns and 2 cups of water. Cover and cook on a low flame till it's done.

Sprouted Moong Khichdi

Mix 1 cup of sprouted moong and 1 cup of rice. Set them aside. Heat 2 tsp ghee in a pan, add a pinch of hing and 1 tsp cumin seeds. Once they splutter, add 2 tbsp dry desiccated coconut, 1 tsp red chilli powder, ½ tsp turmeric, 1 tsp coriander powder and salt to taste. Then, add the sprouts and rice mixture and stir-fry for a few minutes. Add 2 cups of water and cook till it's done. Sprinkle some more coconut and fresh chopped coriander leaves on top and pair with a raita.

Really Rich Khichdi

In a pressure cooker, heat 1 tbsp ghee, add 1 bay leaf, 1 green cardamom pod, 1 clove, a small cinnamon stick and 2 dry red chillies. Sauté 1 tsp of ginger garlic paste and a small finely chopped onion till it's a little brown. Add 2 tbsp tomato purée and cook for 5 minutes. Add some chopped potatoes and stir-fry for a few minutes. Add ½ cup of dal and 1 cup of rice along with a pinch of turmeric powder and dry ginger each. Top it off with 1 tbsp raisins, ½ tsp sugar, salt to taste and 2 cups of water. Mix everything. Add 1 tsp ghee and cook for 2 whistles. Garnish with roasted cashews and almonds and serve with a *paneer* (cottage cheese) or meat curry.

Mutton Khichdi

Heat 2 tbsp ghee in a pressure cooker. Add a pinch of cumin seeds, 2 cloves, 2 cardamom pods and 1 chopped onion. Sauté till the onions are light brown. To this, add 2 chopped green chillies and 1 tsp ginger garlic paste. Toss in 2 tbsp tomato purée, a pinch of turmeric powder, ½ tsp garam masala powder and salt to taste. Cook for 2 minutes. Add ½ cup toor dal and stir-fry for 2–3 minutes. Then, add 1 cup of rice and 2 and ½ cups of water. Add 1 sliced and fried onion and 200 gm cooked (or leftover) mutton. Pressure cook on high heat for 3 whistles and on low heat for 20 minutes more. Garnish with some more fried onions, slit green chillies and cashews. Pair with a chilled raita and serve.

RICE FLOUR (AKKI)

This gluten-free flour is light on the stomach and delivers multiple important nutrients like zinc, calcium and vitamin B6.

Rice Flour (Akki) Roti

In a bowl, add ½ cup chopped leafy vegetables (like, spinach, methi leaves, radish leaves, dill leaves), ½ a chopped onion, ¼ grated radish and carrot each, 2 tbsp fresh coconut, 1 tsp cumin seeds, a pinch of hing, 2 dried red chillies, salt to taste and mix well. Then, add ½ cup rice flour and mix well. Add the necessary amount of water to knead the dough.

Grease a cold tawa with some oil. Spread the dough into a thin layer evenly with your hands. Heat the tawa, pour some oil on the sides. Cover and cook it for 3–4 minutes.

Once the roti is cooked from one side, flip it and cook the other side for 2–3 minutes on high flame. Uncover and let it simmer for a few more minutes on sim until it is cooked through. Pair with a chutney and serve.

BIRYANI AND PILAF

Basic Pilaf

Soak 1 cup of rice in water for 30 minutes. Strain the rice and keep it aside.

Heat ghee or oil in a deep, thick-bottomed pot or pan. Add 2 whole cardamom pods and half an inch of cinnamon. Add 2 thinly sliced onions and sauté on a low flame till they're golden. Crush ½ an inch of ginger, 3–4 garlic pods and 3 green chillies into a paste, add it to the onions and sauté. Add chopped vegetables (½ cup each of carrots, peas and cauliflower) and sauté for 2–3 minutes on a low flame. Add some chopped coriander and mint leaves. Add the rice. Sauté gently for 2 minutes on a low to medium-low flame. Then, pour 2 cups of water to taste. Stir well. Add salt and cover till it is cooked.

Soy Biryani

Cook ½ cup of soy chunks in warm salted water for about 10 minutes. Cook ½ cup of rice and keep it aside. Heat 1 tbsp oil in a pan and add 1 tsp cumin seeds. When they start to splutter, add 1 big sliced onion and 2–3 chopped green chillies. When the onions turn light pink, add the soaked soy chunks, cooked rice, a pinch of turmeric powder, salt to taste and ½ tbsp biryani masala (optional).

Serve with tomato–onion–green chillies raita.

Quick Fix Chicken Biryani

Mix ¼ cup of tomato purée, 1 cup curd, 1 tbsp ginger garlic paste, a few green chillies, 1 tsp red chilli powder, ½ tsp turmeric powder, ½ tsp roasted cumin powder, 1 tsp garam masala powder, ½ tsp coriander powder and salt. Marinate 1 kg chicken pieces in this mixture for 2 hours.

Slice 1 large onion and fry it till it is golden brown. Add the marinated chicken to the onions and cook for 10 minutes Add 1 cup of rice with 1.5 cups of water and a few saffron strands mixed with milk to the cooked chicken mix. Stir gently, bring it to a boil and then cover the pan with a lid. Let it cook on low flame for 15 minutes. Let it sit for 10 minutes without stirring. Garnish with coriander leaves (optional). Serve hot with a curry or cucumber or onion–tomato raita.

(You can make this biryani with potato, cauliflower or mixed vegetables too).

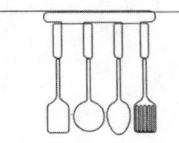

PART 2

The Dal Drawer

There is no doubt that dals are a mainstay of most meals across the country. Every time I dig into a bowl of dal chawal—my go-to dish whenever I don't have time to cook anything else or my mood needs a bit of uplifting—I realize just how ubiquitous dal is. And yet, it is so unappreciated. During the multiple Covid lockdowns, we realized just how handy these kitchen staples can be, as dals are so easy to store and cook. They are also the perfect answer to all our nutritional needs.

The Benefits of Dals

As a nutritionist, I am all for the ubiquitous dals. The benefits of eating them are immense; some of them have been listed below.

- They are a great source of protein (particularly for vegetarians). When combined with cereals (like rice and roti), they deliver complete protein.
- They contain virtually no fat and are low-calorie.
- They provide lots of essential nutrients and antioxidants. They are a good source of potassium, calcium, zinc, niacin and vitamin K.

- They are particularly rich in folate, which is good for the heart because it lowers the homocysteine levels—a serious risk factor for heart disease.
- They are packed with soluble fibre, which helps lower cholesterol levels and reduce the risk of heart disease and stroke. They also keep the digestive tract working efficiently, keeping constipation away.
- Their high fibre content prevents blood sugar levels from rising rapidly after a meal, thus stabilizing the blood sugar levels. They also tend to be low on GI and are good for diabetics too.
- The best thing about dals is that they are extremely versatile; you can make everything from snacks to stews and pilafs to salads using them.
- And, of course, they are super tasty!

FIVE

The Versatile Besan

Most of us usually stock up on besan and that's a good practice. This super fine flour is amazingly versatile and is brilliant for your health too.

THE BENEFITS OF BESAN

The benefits of eating besan, which is made by grinding chana dal, are immense; some of them have been listed below.

- Besan has a lot of soluble fibre, which reduces blood cholesterol levels.
- Besan is also absorbed slowly into the bloodstream, as a result the blood sugar levels rise slowly.
- It has more protein than wheat flour (for example, a single besan *cheela* [a kind of savoury pancake] can give you about 10 gm protein) and has high-satiety value, keeping cravings in check.
- It is gluten-free. So, it also gives us a much-needed break from gluten.

Change How You Cook with Besan

You can always make *kadhi* or cheela or pakoras with besan, but why not experiment with it a little so that you can eat it more often for better health?

Here are a few delicious besan recipes that are also easy to cook.

Besan Halwa

In a pan on a low flame, add ½ tbsp ghee and a pinch of turmeric powder. Then, add 1.5 tbsp besan and stir for 2–3 minutes. Add a few slivered almonds and continue to stir for another 3–4 minutes till the besan is roasted well (deep yellow) and a strong aroma wafts from the pan. Add 1 cup of warm milk and 1 tbsp sugar and stir well. Boil the mixture, add a pinch of crushed pepper and let it boil for another 2 minutes. Once it reaches a thick consistency, serve it warm.

Besan ki Roti

Mix 400 gm besan, 200 gm whole wheat flour, 2 tbsp thinly chopped onions, 1 chopped green chilli, a few fresh coriander and mint leaves, 1 tsp red chilli powder, ½ tsp turmeric powder, a few fresh curry leaves and knead the dough with water. Cook the rotis in desi ghee.

Besan Aloo

Dry roast 4 tbsp of besan and keep it aside. Heat 1 tbsp oil in the pan. Add 2 large boiled and cooled potatoes and bell peppers. Add chilli powder, cumin powder, turmeric and salt to taste. Sprinkle a little water and cover the pan. After 5 minutes, add the roasted besan and ½ tsp amchoor. Mix well to ensure that the besan properly coats the vegetables and cook on a low flame for 5 minutes before serving.

Rajasthani Mirchi Vada

Slit 4 long and thick green chillies, stuff them with salted and mashed boiled potatoes. Make a thick besan batter by mixing

3 tbsp besan with water. Dip the stuffed chillies in a thick besan batter and fry them until they are crisp.

Maharashtrian Pithla

Heat 1 tbsp oil, add a pinch of mustard seeds, let them splutter. Then, add ½ chopped onion, 1 chopped green chilli, a bit of shredded ginger and sauté for 3–4 minutes. In a bowl, mix ½ cup of besan with 2 cups of buttermilk or just water. Add this mixture to the pan. Add a pinch of turmeric, salt to taste and stir till it thickens a bit. Pair with rice. It is perfect for days when you don't have any vegetables at home or just need a change.

Maharashtrian Zunka

This is a dry form of pithla. In a kadai, heat 1 tbsp oil, add mustard seeds, hing and cumin seeds. Sauté 2 cloves of chopped garlic, 2 sliced chillies and 1 chopped onion for 3 minutes. Then, add a pinch of turmeric, chilli powder and salt to taste. Add 1 cup of besan and roast till it turns golden in colour. Pour in 1 cup of water bit by bit. Keep adding water and stirring for about 10 minutes till the besan is cooked. Sprinkle chopped coriander leaves on top. Serve with bajra roti.

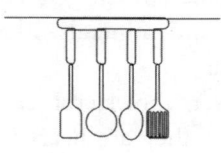

SIX

The Multifaceted Chickpeas

Did you know that chickpeas are basically chana dal with their skin on? They are eaten across the country in most households, albeit in different ways. Almost everyone I know has a nice memory related to chickpeas.

THE BENEFITS OF CHICKPEAS

Chickpeas are really good for you. They are loaded with healthy nutrients. I have listed some of the benefits of eating chickpeas below:

- They are loaded with fibre, which satiate us with less amount of food and effectively curbs the urge to snack.
- They are packed with antioxidants—vitamin C and E, and beta-carotene (which gets converted to vitamin A in the body)—and minerals, like manganese, that are difficult to find.
- They help lower cholesterol and triglycerides in the body. Therefore, they are heart-healthy and help boost our immunity.
- Finally, they are a high tryptophan food. So, they can help calm your mind and lull you into deep sleep.

So, having a cup of cooked chickpeas in some form at least thrice every week is a brilliant idea.

STORY TIME

Ayaan Ali Bangash—a celebrated sarod player and younger son and disciple of the *sarod* maestro Amjad Ali Khan—likes chickpeas a lot. They are an integral part of his diet. Ayaan also has many memories associated with chickpeas because his mum, Subhalakshmi Barua Khan, is from Assam and chickpeas are used in many Assamese dishes, which is the food he grew up with.

The famous *ghugni* is wildly popular as a street food in Assam and West Bengal. It can be prepared as a dry snack or a curry, depending on what you are serving it with. Ayaan shares that his earliest memories of ghugni take him back to Assam trips sometimes even high tea—would be ghugni and *lusi* (Assamese deep-fried flatbread). The fascination about ghugni can also be seen in Bengal, where you have street vendors selling steaming little bowls of ghugni topped with onions, chillies and coriander.

What's more, Ayaan shared that he loves to add a lot of chickpeas in the salads he makes—inspired by the boom in the healthy Mediterranean cuisine, which extensively uses chickpeas.

'I am a humble custodian of an art form that is tied closely to spirituality. The beauty of being a musician is that you will always be a student, as the world of musical knowledge takes several lifetimes to master, if ever! I believe that music and cooking can never be the same, as it's art that you make your own. Something that reflects who you are as a human being,' he said.

Ayaan Ali Bangash's Daliya with Chickpeas

Grind 2 red chillies, 3 cloves garlic, $\frac{1}{2}$ tbsp roasted coriander seeds, $\frac{1}{2}$ tbsp roasted cumin seeds and salt to taste. Pour this paste in a jar, add 1 tbsp lemon juice and 1 tbsp olive oil and shake. Cook 1 cup of daliya (or couscous) and mix in 1 cup of boiled chickpeas 1 chopped tomato and onion each, $\frac{1}{2}$ chopped cucumber and the spice paste prepared earlier.

∞

CHANGE HOW YOU COOK CHICKPEAS

Here are a few delicious chickpea recipes that are also easy to cook.

Quick Vegetable Curry

Heat some oil in a pan and cook 250 gm mixed vegetables—like broccoli, cauliflower, beans, carrots and cherry tomatoes—till they are tender and crisp. Add 1 cup of boiled chickpeas with water and spices, like salt, red chilli powder, coriander powder and garam masala, to taste. Cover and bring to a boil, stirring occasionally. Adjust the seasoning, if required. Remove from heat, garnish with coriander leaves and serve.

Lebanese Salad

Mash 1 cup of leftover chole (or boiled and cooled chickpeas) with 1 potato, adding salt to taste. Turn this mash into mini *tikkis*. Pan-fry them in 1 tbsp oil till they are golden brown. Plate them and add strips of ½ carrot, ½ radish and 1 beetroot to it along with a splash of vinegar. Dig in!

Hummus

Soak 1 cup of chickpeas for 4–5 hours and then pressure cook them for 2–3 whistles (till they become soft enough to grind in a mixer). Let the chickpeas cool before grinding them with 3 garlic cloves, 1 tsp cumin powder, ½ tsp red chilli powder, ¼ cup of sesame seeds and salt to taste. Mix 1 tbsp lemon juice and 1 tbsp olive oil. Serve as a dip with vegetable sticks or as a spread on crackers.

Lemon Chickpea Pasta Soup

Heat ½ tbsp olive oil, add ½ a diced onion and carrot each and 2 cloves of minced garlic. Sauté for 5 minutes till the vegetables are cooked. Pour in 3 cups of water along with salt and pepper to taste and boil. Then, add ½ cup of boiled chickpeas, ¼ cup of pasta and 1 bay leaf. Simmer for 10 minutes till the pasta is cooked. Add a few leaves of chopped spinach and 50 gm shredded chicken (optional). Finally, stir in 1 tbsp lemon juice after switching off the gas and serve.

Skinny Chickpea Salad

In a medium bowl, whisk together 1 tbsp olive oil, 1 tbsp lemon juice, 2 cloves of crushed garlic, 1 cup boiled chickpeas and crushed red pepper and salt to taste. Cover and allow the chickpeas to marinate for about 30 minutes at room temperature. Add any green leafy vegetable at hand (lettuce, baby spinach, cabbage, etc.), a handful of steamed French beans and 1 diced cucumber. Mix and enjoy!

Roasted Chickpeas

Pat 30 gm of cooked chickpeas dry and toss them in a bowl with 1 tbsp oil, ½ tsp cumin, ½ tsp oregano and salt. Spread them on a rimmed baking sheet. Bake at 204 °C for 25 to 30 minutes, stirring once or twice until they are light brown and crunchy. Let them cool on the baking sheet for 15 minutes before serving.

Chickpea, Vegetables and Potato Hash

Combine 1 boiled potato, 30 gm spinach, 1 chopped onion, 10 gm ginger, 1 tsp curry powder and salt to taste in a large bowl. Heat 1 tbsp oil in a pan, add the potato mixture and press into a layer. Cook without stirring for about 3 to 5 minutes until the bottom is crispy and golden brown. In a bowl, mix ½ cup of boiled chickpeas and 50 gm shredded zucchini. Press this into an even layer on top of the potatoes. Create 2 wells in the layers. On the side, break 2 eggs, separate their yolks and slip 1 egg yolk into each of the two wells. Cover and cook until the yolks are set before digging in.

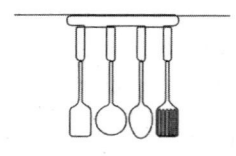

SEVEN

Kickass Kala Chana

We are all mostly familiar with *kala chana* (Bengal gram or garbanzo beans). It is cooked in most households in some form or the other. In many South Indian temples, the *sundal prasad* (a preparation of kala chana made as an offering to God) is kala chana neatly served in a bowl made out of dried leaves (called *dhonne* in Kannada). Kala chana is also traditionally cooked during Navratri as part of the prasad during the Ashtami or Navami *puja*. Ayurveda actually considers kala chana to be *agneya*, which means it is not only a metabolism booster but also helps remove toxins due to its high fibre content.

THE BENEFITS OF KALA CHANA

Kala chana is a nutritional powerhouse. The benefits of eating kala chana are immense. I have listed some of them below.

- Besides being a great source for protein for vegetarians, it delivers lots of fibre that helps regulate your blood sugar level.
- It is also loaded with nutrients like iron, copper, phosphate, magnesium, manganese and zinc, all of which are good for boosting your immune system and heart health.
- It is also high in calcium and vitamin K, both of which keep our bones strong.

- The phytoestrogens in kala chana lower the risk of breast cancer and help keep our cholesterol and triglyceride levels down too.

CHANGE HOW YOU COOK KALA CHANA

Here are a few delicious kala chana recipes that are also easy to cook.

Desi Chaat

Wash and soak ½ cup kala chana overnight in water. The morning after, pressure cook it. Wait for 1 whistle on high and then leave on low gas for 25–30 minutes.

Mix the boiled kala chana with 1 boiled and chopped potato. Toss in 1 tbsp roasted sunflower seeds, some roasted chana, 2 tbsp yoghurt, seeds from ½ a pomegranate and 1 chopped cucumber to make a chaat-like salad. Drizzle ½ tbsp tamarind sauce on top and serve.

Super Quick Tangy Chana Mix

Mix sprouted (or boiled) kala chana, and 1 chopped apple and tomato each in a bowl. Add salt to taste along with a generous squeeze of lemon or tamarind chutney. Mix and enjoy!

Kala Chana Hummus

Blend 1 cup of boiled kala chana with 4 crushed garlic cloves, 2 tbsp roasted white sesame seeds, 4 ice cubes, 2 dried red chillies and 1 tbsp lemon juice in a grinder. Eat it as a dip or spread it on a cracker or toast.

Chana Pumpkin

In a pan with some heated oil, add ½ tsp each cumin seeds, turmeric, red chilli, 1 chopped green chilli, ½ inch ginger, 1 cup or 250 gm boiled kala chana and some chopped pumpkin. Add a splash of water, cover and cook till the pumpkin is soft. Sprinkle salt and amchoor. Garnish with crumbled feta cheese or paneer (optional) on top and dig in.

Kala Chana Sundal

Dry roast 2 tsp each of urad and chana dals. Cool and grind with 1 tsp of whole coriander seeds. Set it aside. Heat 1 tbsp coconut oil, temper with a pinch of mustard seeds, hing and few curry leaves. Add the dry masala and 1 tbsp jaggery to the oil. Stirring briskly, add 1 cup of boiled chana with a couple of spoons of water and salt to taste. Top it off with some fresh coconut. Stir and cook for a couple of minutes before serving.

Easiest Kadala Curry

In a pan, sauté 50 gm fresh coconut, 1 sliced onion, 1 dried red chilli and 1 tsp garam masala. Grind 1 green chilli, a few peppercorns, 2 tsp coriander powder, 4 garlic cloves and 100 gm fresh coconut. Add this paste to the pan. Then, add 1 cup of boiled chana with water to the curry along with salt. Cover and cook on sim for 10 minutes before serving.

Chana and Lauki

In a pan, heat 1 tbsp oil and temper a pinch of mustard and cumin seeds each, a pinch of hing, a few curry leaves and 2 sliced green chillies. Add ½ tsp turmeric, 1 small chopped bottle gourd and 1 tsp salt to the pan. Cover and cook for 5 minutes. Then, add 1 cup of boiled kala chana, mix well and cook for a minute. Garnish with 50 gm fresh or dried coconut and serve.

Puja Kala Chana

Heat 1 tbsp oil and temper 1 tsp of cumin seeds, 1 tsp each of turmeric, salt, red chilli powder, roasted cumin powder and 2 tsp of coriander powder in it. Add 1 cup of boiled kala chana and 1 tsp of amchoor and mix well. Garnish with some coriander leaves. Pair with puri and halwa.

Roti and Palak-Chana Mix

Heat 2 tsp ghee in a pan and add a pinch of mustard and cumin seeds and hing. Stir-fry 1 sliced onion, 2 sliced green chillies and 100 gm torn up palak till it is soft. Add 1 cup of boiled kala chana, and salt and garam masala to taste and cook with a lid on for a few minutes. Then, add 2 roughly torn-up rotis or some noodles or pasta (leftover will also do) to the mix and cook for 2–3 minutes. Garnish with fresh coriander and red chilli flakes and dig in.

Kala Chana Kebab

Mash 2 boiled potatoes (or sweet potatoes) and 1 cup of boiled kala chana. Add 1 finely chopped onion, a bit of ginger and 2 green chillies. Add salt, *kasuri methi* (dried fenugreek leaves) and amchoor powder to taste along with 2 tbsp rice flour. Shape the mash in the form of kebabs and pan-fry on both sides in a little oil, flipping until they are crisp and brown on both sides. Serve hot!

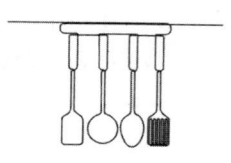

EIGHT

Lobia: The Hidden Gem

Lobia or black-eyed peas are the unpopular cousin of the more widely eaten rajma. However, considering its health benefits, we must make it a part of our regular meals.

THE BENEFITS OF LOBIA

There are many benefits to eating lobia. I have listed some of them below.

- It delivers a lot of folate and other B vitamins along with vitamin A, which is a vision-enhancing nutrient. When you mix lobia up with other vitamin-A-rich foods like carrot, spinach, broccoli, it is also great for healthy skin. It is also an antioxidant that helps boost our immunity.
- Lobia contains the trace mineral manganese, which protects mitochondria, the structures inside cells that produce energy, along with being an antioxidant.
- It is gut friendly, as it is loaded with soluble fibre that binds itself to cholesterol and makes it disposable. Besides, it protects us from several intestinal disorders and keeps constipation away.
- It also helps maintain healthy cholesterol levels by preventing cholesterol from being absorbed into our bloodstream.

- The wonderful combination of protein and fibre make it a low GI food. Therefore, it is good for those who want to lose weight and is safe for diabetics too.
- The potassium in lobia is great to balance the excess sodium in our diet and keep our blood pressure under control. Potassium also helps nurture the nervous system, enhance muscle strength and metabolism and keep bones strong.

CHANGE HOW YOU COOK LOBIA

There are many interesting ways to eat lobia, besides just making a lobia curry—think stews, soups, salads and so on. In fact, this seemingly bland lentil is very versatile and pairs well with most foods (potatoes, rice, tuna and ham, in particular). Here are a few delicious lobia recipes that are also easy to cook.

Lobia Kebab

In a non-stick pan, heat 1 tsp ghee and sauté 1 inch of finely chopped ginger and 2 green chillies for a minute. Temper half tsp of cumin seeds in it and then add ½ cup of boiled lobia, salt to taste and sauté for 2–3 minutes.

Soak 2 slices of bread in water and squeeze them out. Transfer the cooked lobia onto these 2 slices. Sprinkle garam masala powder and coriander leaves on top. Mix well. Shape the lobia mixture into tikkis and shallow-fry on both sides till they are golden brown. Serve with a chutney of your choice.

Lemony Lobia

Boil ½ cup lobia with a little salt. Drain, cool and blend it. In a pan, stir-fry 1 tbsp sesame or olive oil, 2 cloves of sliced garlic and 1 chopped Thai chilli (bird's eye chilli). Add mashed lobia,

1 tbsp black bean sauce, 1 tbsp dark soy sauce, 1 tbsp lemon juice and 1 tbsp vegetable stock or water. Stir in 1 tsp cornflour. Garnish with a few leaves of fresh basil and serve.

Aloo-Lobia Thechwani

Heat 1 tbsp oil in a pressure cooker, add 1 tsp each of cumin and mustard seeds. Add 1 tsp each of chopped garlic and ginger and half a chopped onion. Sauté on low heat for 3–4 minutes. Add 1 finely chopped tomato, 2 boiled and chopped potatoes, ½ cup of soaked (for a few hours) and drained lobia, salt to taste, ½ tsp garam masala and ½ tsp coriander powder. Add 1 cup of water and pressure cook for 2 whistles on high flame and on sim for 7–8 minutes. Garnish with fresh coriander leaves and serve with roti.

Simple Lobia Salad

Toss ½ cup of boiled lobia with a finely chopped onion, tomato and cucumber. Sprinkle some roasted cumin powder, salt and chaat masala. Squeeze some lemon juice. Top with a boiled egg (or some panned strips) and serve.

Beans Bruschetta

Mash 1 cup of boiled lobia and mix 3 tbsp curd to it. Add mustard sauce, salt, dried rosemary, pepper to taste along with 1 tsp oil. Spread the mixture on a bread or cracker, top it with lettuce, sliced cucumber and tomato. Serve grilled or chilled.

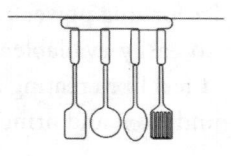

NINE

Sattu: An Indian Superfood

While curating a menu for a superfoods festival for a pan-India cafe chain, everyone was surprised when I insisted on putting sattu on the ingredient list. However, we ended up putting two dishes made from sattu on the menu. Convincing the brand was easy enough once I began rattling off the multiple benefits of this ubiquitous yet completely understated, uniquely Indian superfood.

Some people are aware of how good this ingredient is, and that is why they eat it almost every day, especially in the rural hinterlands of Bihar, Punjab, Madhya Pradesh, Uttar Pradesh, Orissa and West Bengal. In fact, folk tales suggest that it was a favourite food of Shivaji when he was engaged in full-scale guerrilla warfare against the Mughals and their allies.

Today's generation, though, has decided to simply ignore sattu, and most tag it as the poor man's protein. I don't get this—protein is protein, isn't it? Besides, this is an extremely self-defeating mindset to have in a country like ours, where most people don't manage to consume enough protein. Perhaps we need a marketing blitz for this power-packed ancient instant food of India, which is so easily available around us.

Meanwhile, though, I feel like creating awareness about sattu might also open some minds to it and bring it back on our plates.

THE BENEFITS OF SATTU

I have listed some of the immense benefits of eating sattu below.

- It provides instant energy and is a brilliant source of good quality vegetarian protein. In many households that are aware of its nutritional value, 2 tsp of sattu is mandatory for every child every day, as it helps build their muscle mass.
- It has a lot of fibre and works wonders for those who are suffering from gas, acidity and constipation too.
- It has a low GI. So, it is good for diabetics.
- It is low on sodium so it's good for hypertensive people as well.
- It contains calcium (which makes it good for our bones), iron, manganese, magnesium and vitamins A and C.
- It is an effective antidote to sweltering summer heat, as it is naturally cooling.
- Finally, it has a long shelf life.

One thing to keep in mind about sattu is that it has a high calorific value (100 gm of sattu has close to 400 calories). The original method of cooking sattu involves drying roasting chana dal in sand (the way peanuts were roasted originally), straining it through a sieve and pounding the roasted chana to a powder. Traditionally, sattu has always been made with chana but some people add some chickpeas too for a twist in flavour. In Punjab, barley sattu is more popular. You no longer have to put in the hard work of making sattu, though, because both chana and barley versions of sattu are easily available commercially.

Sattu is our very own indigenous, completely natural and safe protein powder, perfect for good health and weight loss. And it's incredibly delicious. It's about time sattu got its due.

CHANGE HOW YOU COOK SATTU

Sattu is a very versatile ingredient and can be eaten in multiple ways. Here are a few delicious sattu recipes that are also easy to cook.

Sattu Sherbet, 4 Ways

- **Sweet sherbet:** If you like your drinks sweet, just mix jaggery powder and sattu and blend with some water (or coconut water) to form a smooth paste. Add chilled water to the mixture along with lemon juice and mint leaves and serve.
- **Savoury sattu:** Follow the same process you did for the sweet sherbet but skip the jaggery and add a pinch of black salt and chaat masala instead. Your instant energy drink is ready!
- **Protein power drink:** Mix sattu with buttermilk. Garnish with a few mint leaves, a pinch of black salt and chaat masala.
- **Masala sattu:** Add the juice of 1 lemon to coconut water, sprinkle some black salt, some fresh coriander leaves and a bit of roasted cumin powder and mix with 2 tbsp sattu.

Sattu Paratha

Knead 30 gm sattu flour with mustard oil, some grated onion, grated ginger, green chillies, amchoor, salt and chilli powder to taste. Shape the dough into lemon-sized balls. Roll a tomato-sized ball of 50 gm whole-wheat dough into a roti. Place the sattu ball in the centre, gather the edges of the dough and seal the sattu into the roti. Press gently into a thick disc and roll out the paratha. Cook both sides on a hot tawa. Serve with curd or buttermilk. You can also stuff the paratha with boiled potatoes, dals, paneer or any leftover sabzi.

Tip: Try having sattu paratha with chicken curry. It's amazing!

Sattu Cheela

Mix 1 cup of sattu with ½ cup *suji* (semolina) and ½ cup besan. Add salt, some coriander or mint leaves and mix with 1 cup of curd and water as needed until a smooth batter forms. Spread on a heated, greased pan, drizzle oil around the sides and cook on both sides until golden brown. Pair with mint chutney and buttermilk.

Sattu Porridge

In a pan, add 2 tbsp sattu, 1 cup water and 1 tbsp sugar and mix well. Cook this for 3–4 minutes till the mixture thickens, ensuring that no lumps are formed. Add 1 cup of milk and cook for just a minute. Add some chopped dry fruits on top and dig in.

Sattu Pakora

Mix 1 cup of sattu with finely chopped onions, green chilli, a pinch of turmeric powder, salt and pepper powder. Gradually add water until the mixture reaches the consistency of a batter. Shallow or deep-fry like a pakora.

Quick Sattu Breakfast

Mix sattu with sugar and cold water and breakfast will be ready in a jiffy.

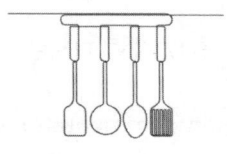

TEN

Toor and Moong: Everyday Super Dals

Moong dal and toor dal are the most cooked dals in many households. Our palates are used to them because we have grown up eating them. In a way, they are the ultimate comfort foods.

The flip side of this comfort is the boredom that comes with familiarity.

But I urge you to not give up on these delicious and healthy dals. Moong dal is known to reduce cholesterol. It is also a great summer food because it cools the body during the months of heat.

Toor dal is a famously heart-healthy food because it contains potassium, which is a vasodilator (food that keeps blood pressure in check), along with phosphorus and magnesium, both of which help maintain a normal heartbeat. Incorporate these healthy and comforting dals in your diet right away!

∞

STORY TIME

Charu Sharma, an Indian commentator, compere, quizmaster and director of the famous pro Kabaddi League, has an interesting story to tell. During his early years in Ajmer, when he was studying in Mayonnaise College, a few family friends asked his mother what she was feeding the 8-year-old Charu. They wanted to know how he was doing so well in sports. 'She was embarrassed. We were, after all, a family of modest means. So, she told them what came to her mind first—that she fed me mixed dal every day. I am in my early sixties now and I am still a vegetarian. My mother has passed away and that dal recipe has gone with her but, thanks to that, I still love all dals. I am terribly unfussy about food and I am actually exactly the opposite of a foodie. But dals are a must for me as a reasonable source of protein. No meal for me, even today, is complete without dal,' Charu shared.

∽

In India, of course, dals are omnipresent. A foodie friend tells me that in the Bengali cuisine, dals begin appearing right from breakfast, Bihar swears by ghugni (black gram or dried yellow or white peas coked in a gravy) and sattu, and everyone has surely tasted Rajasthan's tasty *gatte ki sabzi*.

∽

Ashok Parija, Senior Advocate and Advocate General of Orissa, shares that even after leaving Odisha, an Odia always craves *dalma* with rice or roti. 'I have grown up seeing dalma being cooked 5 days a week in my house. Basically, it is a nutritious dish made with moong or toor dal and an assortment of vegetables, typically brinjal, raw banana, raw papaya and pumpkins. So, this dish is packed with proteins from the dal and minerals and vitamins from the vegetables. The dalma is topped off with an aromatic tempering made in desi ghee with roasted cumin seeds and chilli powder, which acts as a catalyst to bring out its best taste. Thus, it is a perfect combination of taste and health,' he shared.

∽

The best part is you don't have to do anything extra to get these dals back on your menus. Here is a selection of a few delicious recipes that are also easy to cook.

Mutton Dal

Boil 100 gm yellow moong dal in a pressure cooker with water, 100 gm tomatoes, 1 bay leaf, 1 inch cinnamon stick, a few curry leaves and salt to taste. Once cooked, mash the dal and set it aside.

In a pressure cooker, heat 1 tbsp oil, add 1 sliced onion, a few mint leaves and cook till the onion becomes translucent. Add 50 gm mutton chunks, ½ tsp turmeric powder, ½ tsp red chilli powder, 1 tbsp ginger garlic paste, a pinch of garam masala powder and some water to the pan. Cook on high heat for 1 whistle, then on low gas for 30 minutes till the mutton gets cooked.

Stir in the mashed dal with the mutton curry and cook for 5–10 minutes. Pair with rotis.

Refreshing Dal-Beetroot Medley

Boil ½ cup of green moong (soaked for 2 hours) till it is cooked but still has a bit of crunch. To the cooled moong, add 1 shredded beetroot, 1 chopped spring onion, roasted peanuts or walnuts and season with salt and pepper. Drizzle 1 tsp shredded ginger, ½ tsp mustard, 1 tsp oil and 1 tsp vinegar (mixed well) over the salad. Chill and serve.

Hyderabadi Khatti Dal

Cook 1 cup of toor dal with 3 cups of water, a pinch of turmeric powder, 1 cup chopped tomato, 1 tsp ginger garlic paste, a pinch of red chilli powder, 2 slit green chillies and salt to taste. Then, add 1 tsp tamarind pulp and cook for 5 minutes.

Temper 2–3 garlic cloves, 2 dry red chillies, a few curry leaves, 1 tsp cumin seeds and ½ tsp mustard seeds in 1 tsp oil and pour over the dal. Enjoy it with rice.

Gujarati Dal Roti

Soak 1 cup of toor dal for 1 hour in very little water. Add the soaked dal to a heated pan and cook till all the leftover liquid has dried. Stir in 1 tbsp sugar. Then, add 1 tbsp cardamom powder and ½ tsp poppy seeds to the cooked dal. Let the mixture cool.

Meanwhile, make a dough out of wheat flour, a little oil and water. Make small roti-like circles from the dough, place some of the cooked dal as stuffing in the centre of each tiny roti before sealing it shut. Roll out a roti from this stuffed dough ball and cook on a hot tawa. Apply a little ghee on both sides. Serve with raita.

Dal Soup

To 1.5 cups of water, add 2 tbsp of any dal and boil it till the dal is cooked. Pour a tadka of just 1 tbsp chopped onion, 1 green chilli, lots of cumin seeds, salt to taste and a chopped tomato (optional). Squeeze a bit of lemon on top. Serve piping hot.

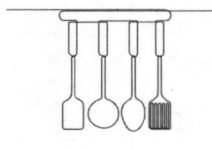

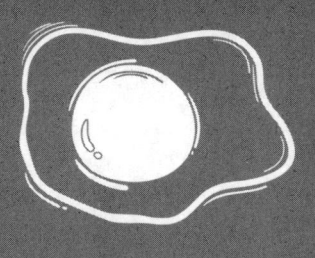

PART 3

Protein Power

When we talk about critical deficiencies that afflict Indians, along with iron and calcium, protein deficiency tops the list. Unfortunately, though, most of us don't give protein much thought. The common thinking is that protein is important only for bodybuilders or those who exercise a lot, whereas the fact is that many of us tend to be protein-deficient, as we don't eat enough good quality protein.

The Benefits of Protein

The benefits of eating enough protein are immense. I've listed some of them below.

- Protein is very important for us because, unlike fats and carbohydrates, it is not stored in the body and its deficiency can deplete our muscle mass.
- Every body part is made up of protein. So, it is necessary for maintenance, upkeep and regeneration of all our body cells and organs—right from hair to hormones, antibodies to nerves, and haemoglobin to bones.
- Protein-deficient diets, coupled with our sedentary

- lifestyles, can hugely impact muscle health, leading to multiple long-term problems as well.
- Sufficient protein is important to avoid weakness, fatigue, inefficient day-to-day functioning and to prevent metabolic syndrome, impaired muscle function and an increased risk of infectious diseases.

So, it is important to take protein seriously. Eating a balanced diet is the way to ensure sufficient protein in our diet. Look closely at your plate to check whether you are eating enough high-quality, complete protein. Meats, eggs, dairy, seafood, nuts, seeds, legumes and beans deliver a good amount of protein. Some grains, like quinoa, bajra, buckwheat and amaranth, also have protein, as do some vegetables like beetroot, peas and French beans.

ELEVEN

Eggscellent!

Eggs are one of the most easily accessible, complete foods. They are versatile enough to be eaten in any meal, be it breakfast, lunch, dinner or even as a snack. That is precisely why they are cooked and eaten in every country of the world. I am a huge egg lover and eat it every day.

STORY TIME

Romi Dev, an entrepreneur, agrees with me. She said that eggs are a staple part of her family's diet and are eaten every day. 'I am a total egg person and can eat them in any form. My daughter eats her chilly cheese omelette before work almost thrice a week and whatever Kapil is having for breakfast, a crisp fried egg is essential. We have a special tiny frying pan for fried eggs that accommodates up to 3 eggs at a time. The trick is to heat the oil till it's smoking, break the eggs into it and cover to cook. Then, the whites crisp up and the yolk remains gooey. We sprinkle rock salt and red chilli flakes before taking it out of the pan,' she shared.

For Romi, in winter, a constant is egg with peas. 'I simply cook the peas in a pan with only ginger and green chillies cut into strips. The peas, especially Jaipur peas, are so soft and sweet in winter that they cook immediately. Then, I just break the eggs over the peas and cover the pan. This way they set over the peas and all I need to do is slide the dish onto a plate and dig in,' she shared.

༄

If we took a vote for the most maligned food over the last decade or two, eggs will win hands down. They have faced a lot of flak and have been painted as a cholesterol-increasing, heart-harming devil in incessant but baseless media reports. But, thankfully, all that is in the past now. Fat is no longer a demon and cholesterol from food sources has been declared perfectly safe to consume. So, eggs are out of the woods and are considered safe to eat again.

THE BENEFITS OF EGGS

The fact is that eggs are more than just safe. They are a complete food and pack quite a nutritional punch. The benefits of eating eggs are immense; some of them have been listed below.

- Eggs deliver protein, which builds and maintains muscles; vitamin A, which is important for eyesight; B vitamins, which are essential for efficient metabolism; vitamin E, which is a powerful antioxidant; and even some vitamin D, which is rare to find in food sources and is important for the development and maintenance of healthy bones, among other things.
- They also contain calcium, which builds strong bones and teeth; phosphorus, which is important for healthy bones and teeth; iron, which carries oxygen to muscles;

zinc, which helps the body grow; and selenium, which is an important antioxidant.
- They are low in calories. An egg delivers only between 60–80 calories and you can actually make a decent, satisfying meal out of just 2 eggs and some accompanying vegetables. The math adds up to make eggs pretty friendly for our weight!
- They are a high-satiety food. Eggs are loaded with protein (delivering about 6 gm per egg), which makes us feel full and reduces our appetite.
- They also have good fats, which keep our metabolism running and our weight in check.

Note: A myth that needs to be busted is that one should only have egg whites. The fact is that the whites have about half of an egg's protein content, almost all of its sodium and only trace amounts of other nutrients. In fact, the nutrition in albumen (egg white) is fairly pointless, particularly when contrasted with the yolk, which is loaded with nutritional goodness.

So, please eat eggs whole, particularly because the yolks deliver lutein and zeaxanthin, two carotenoids that are crucial for eye health and protect the eye from the damage caused by ultraviolet light. Yolks also contain choline, a dietary component essential for the normal functioning of all cells, particularly brain cells. So, eggs can actually help boost your memory.

CHANGE HOW YOU COOK EGGS

There are more ways to have eggs than just egg fry, omelette or boiled eggs. Here are a few delicious egg recipes that are also easy to cook.

Egg Salad

If you keep extra boiled eggs handy in the fridge, this recipe is for you. Toss 2 boiled and chopped eggs, ½ cup of boiled and finely diced carrot, ½ finely diced cucumber, ½ cup of spring onions, along with any other vegetables you have handy together. Mix 2 cups of boiled and mashed potatoes into this mixture. Add salt and pepper to taste along with 2 tbsp low-fat mayonnaise or hung curd. Chill and eat with a side of stir-fried greens.

Spinach and Eggs, 2 Ways

- To 2 tsp heated oil, add 1 cup of chopped tomatoes and a few cloves of crushed garlic, and cook for about 4 minutes. Transfer this mixture to a bowl. In the same pan, in 1 tsp oil, sauté 100 gm spinach leaves and ½ a chopped onion with a pinch of red chilli flakes. Flatten the cooked spinach in the pan. Scatter blistered tomatoes over it, season with salt and pepper. Pour two beaten eggs over the spinach and tomatoes and scramble the eggs on low heat. Dig in!
- Heat 1 tbsp oil, add 1 chopped onion and cook till it is translucent. Add 200 gm chopped spinach and toss for 1–2 minutes until it begins to wilt. Let it cool. Beat 2 eggs, add the spinach and onion mix, then add 50 gm feta cheese and salt and pepper to taste. Pour the mix into a heated frying pan after brushing a little oil on it. Cover and cook till the eggs are done.

Shakshuka

Heat 1 tbsp olive oil in a pan and add ½ a chopped onion, 2 cloves of garlic and 2 finely chopped red bell peppers. Cook for 5 minutes. Add 2 large chopped tomatoes and 1 tbsp tomato sauce. Season with a pinch each of cumin powder, chilli powder, sugar and paprika. Make two wells in the sauce and crack 1 egg into each. Top with some feta cheese. Cover and cook for 5 minutes and take off the heat while the eggs are a bit runny. Season with salt and pepper before serving.

Eggs Frittata

Add 1 chopped spring onion, 1 tbsp chopped red bell pepper, salt and pepper and 3 thin potato wafers to 2 whisked eggs and set the mixture aside for 5 minutes till the wafers soak up some of the egg and become soggy. Heat 1 tsp oil in a pan, pour the egg and wafer mix onto it, keep the flame low. Cover and cook for 2 minutes on low flame. Top it off with 4 more wafers and 1 tbsp yellow bell pepper, pressing them down gently. Cover and cook. Flip for a minute to brown lightly. Serve wafer side up.

Egg Pakora

Peel and cut 2 boiled eggs into two halves and sprinkle some salt and pepper on them. In a bowl, take 2 tbsp besan and add salt and chilli powder to taste. Pour water into this until a thick batter forms. Heat oil in a kadai. Dip each egg piece in the batter and deep- or air-fry till golden brown on medium flame. Eat with tomato or coriander–mint chutney.

Egg Dog

In small bowl, beat together an egg, a little milk, salt and pepper. Cook on a non-stick pan smeared with oil. When the egg is almost done, top with grated cheese and a slice of ham. Then, slowly roll the omelette (like a hot dog) and slide it onto a hot dog bun.

Baked Eggs

Butter the base of a baking dish and place two coarsely chopped tomatoes and a few garlic pods in it. Season with salt and pepper to taste. Break two eggs over the mixture. Sprinkle paprika, oregano and chilli flakes and bake the dish for 10 minutes in a preheated oven at 190 °C. Serve hot!

Masala Deviled Eggs

Cut 2 hard-boiled eggs, remove and mash their yolks with 1 tsp each of tomato and Tabasco sauces, season with salt and pepper and fill the yolk mix back into the empty egg whites. Meanwhile, in a pan, cook a sauce with ½ a chopped onion and tomato each and 1 tsp ginger garlic paste, season with spices to taste. Then place the devilled eggs in it, cover and cook for 2–3 minutes. This tastes lovely with paratha

Eggs Florentine

In a pan, heat 10 gm butter and toss in 2–3 chopped garlic cloves. Stir-fry about 100 gm of washed and cleaned spinach leaves in the hot pan for a minute. Meanwhile, boil some water in a fresh pan, break 2 eggs onto a big spoon and gently slide them into the hot water. When the eggs have poached for 2 minutes, remove them. Layer the spinach on a toasted slice of bread, place the eggs over it and enjoy!

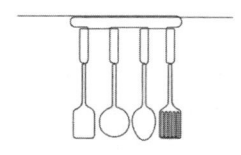

TWELVE

Peppy Paneer

Paneer is a ubiquitous ingredient. It's cooked and eaten in almost every household, especially in primarily vegetarian kitchens.

STORY TIME

Tarun Sibal, a chef-entrepreneur, has a funny memory to share about paneer. 'I am a typical Punjabi lad and in my house, whenever paneer would be made, the funny part was that there was no specific recipe or dish name. For example, if I would come back from school and ask what's for lunch, the answer was simple: there's paneer for lunch. There was no specific name for the dish. Paneer meant paneer. It was only when I became older, I realized that many different dishes could be made from paneer,' he shared. Today, he loves the *jhatphat* paneer bhurjee the most. 'And to make it interesting, I add a little burrata and tomato chutney on top,' he shared.

THE BENEFITS OF PANEER

Most people I know love paneer but are kind of bored of regular paneer dishes. However, eating paneer is immensely beneficial. I've listed some of the benefits below.

- Paneer is a brilliant source of body-building protein as well as bone and teeth building calcium for vegetarians.
- It contains the right amount of potassium and sodium, which keep the blood pressure stable and the heart healthy.
- The magnesium in paneer boosts immunity, and folate helps prevent anaemia.
- It is also a high-satiety food that keeps us full for a long time.

CHANGE HOW YOU COOK PANEER

The best part is that paneer is loved almost universally. It is an amazingly versatile ingredient that can be eaten in multiple ways.

Here are a few delicious paneer recipes that are also easy to cook.

Grilled Peri Peri Paneer Salad with Vegetables

To make peri peri sauce, grind 3 dry red chillies, ½ red pepper, 1 tbsp vinegar, 4–5 cloves of garlic, 1 tbsp oil and salt and pepper to taste. Coat 200 gm sliced paneer in peri peri sauce and pan-fry on both sides till the pieces are golden brown. Set this aside. Stir-fry 10 button mushrooms, 100 gm broccoli and 100 gm red and yellow pepper each. Season with salt, pepper and a dollop of the peri peri sauce. Pair the vegetables with the cooked paneer and enjoy!

Paneer Stuffed Besan Cheela

In a bowl, mix 100 gm besan, a pinch of ajwain, 1 tsp each of red chilli powder and coriander powder, ½ tsp garam masala and salt to taste. To this, add 2 tbsp curd and a little water bit by bit to make a thin batter. To make the stuffing, mix 100 gm crumbled paneer, 1 chopped onion, 2 chopped green chillies, ½ tsp red chilli powder and cumin powder each and some coriander leaves and set aside.

Coat a heated pan with some oil, pour a ladle of the batter and spread it into a circle. Cook on both sides for about 2–3 minutes each. Place 2–3 tbsp of stuffing on one side of the cheela and roll. Enjoy with mint and coriander chutney.

Spicy Snacky Paneer

Whisk together 2 tbsp of curd, 1 tbsp of ginger garlic paste, 1 tbsp oil, a pinch of turmeric and salt and pepper to taste. Marinate cubes of 100 gm paneer in this mixture for an hour. Then, place these in the oven and roast for 15 minutes. When it is done, garnish with herbs of your choice and serve.

Pan-fried Red Paneer

To 1 cup of curd, add 1 tsp each of coriander leaves, amchoor powder, garam masala, red chilli powder and kasuri methi, 1 tbsp sesame or olive oil, 2 tbsp *maida* (refined wheat flour) and salt to taste. Coat paneer pieces with this mixture and pan-fry on both sides. Roll in lettuce leaves and enjoy.

Naan Pizza

Blend 50 gm of paneer with 2 tsp milk cream. Spread it over a naan or paratha. Spread 1 tbsp of mint–coriander chutney. Add slices of capsicum, onion and ham (optional). Drizzle a little olive oil on top and grill on medium heat for 7–8 minutes until the vegetables have slightly browned. Cut into slices and serve hot.

Paneer and Fruit Sandwich

On a thin slice of brown bread, spread 100 gm of crumbled paneer that has been lightly seasoned with salt and pepper. Place slices of mango, melon or strawberries on top along with some sliced red pepper. Top it off with another slice of brown bread and dig in.

Green and White Delight

Place a thick, fresh square of paneer on a slice of bread slathered with a spicy coriander chutney. Sprinkle salt and red chilli on it. Place a few slices of onion rings, thin-sliced slivers of 1 green chilli, ¼ chopped green capsicum, ½ chopped carrot and ¼ chopped cabbage over the paneer. Top with another slice slathered with coriander chutney and serve.

Apple Dairy Mix

Mix 1 grated apple with 100 gm paneer. Add a few chopped walnuts, raisins and 1 dried fig to it. Place the mixture on a slice of whole wheat bread and dig in.

Stuffed Paneer French Toast

Mix 50 gm crumbled paneer with 1 chopped onion and tomato each, 2 chopped green chillies and salt to taste. Spread butter on 1 slice of bread. Layer the paneer stuffing over the bread. Top with another bread slice layered with butter. Beat 1 egg with salt and pepper to taste. Thoroughly coat the sandwich in the egg mixture. Cook on a heated pan till golden brown on both sides.

Paneer Tikka, 2 Ways

- **Red paneer tikka:** Chop 1 onion and 1 capsicum into 1 inch pieces, cube 200 gm paneer and set aside. In a bowl, whisk together 200 gm hung curd or Greek yoghurt, add 1 tsp each of ginger garlic paste, red chilli powder, coriander powder, turmeric, cumin powder, amchoor powder, chaat masala, black pepper powder, 1.5 tbsp lemon juice, 1 tbsp mustard oil and a pinch of salt. Add the cut paneer and vegetables to the marinade. Cover and keep it in the fridge for at least an hour. Grill in the oven at 200 °C for about 12–14 minutes. Serve with green chutney.
- **Green tikka:** Blend 100 gm fresh coriander leaves, 20 gm garlic, 100 gm mint leaves and a few green chillies with 2 tbsp thick curd. Add 1 tsp each of chilli powder, turmeric, cumin powder, amchoor powder, chaat masala, a pinch of garam masala, 1 tsp besan, 1 tsp lemon juice, 1 tsp mustard oil and salt to taste. Marinate cubed paneer and chopped onion and capsicum in it. Refrigerate for an hour before grilling in the oven at 200 °C for 12–14 minutes.

Lettuce Paneer Rolls

Wash 10 lettuce leaves well and spread them out on a plate. Stir-fry 200 gm paneer with ¼ each of an onion and tomato and 1 green chilli in 1 tbsp oil. Roll the cooked paneer (you can also use paneer tikka as the stuffing, find the recipe above) in the lettuce. Steam for 10 minutes and serve.

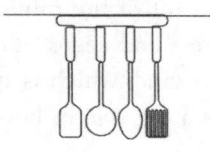

THIRTEEN

Fall in Love with Tofu

It is important to vary our protein choices so that we don't get bored with a source. If you are a vegetarian and are tired of eating paneer, you can try tofu. Not only is it delicious and super healthy, it is also extremely versatile and can be cooked in multiple ways.

THE BENEFITS OF TOFU

Eating tofu has immense benefits. Some of them have been listed below.

- If you are looking to perk up your dull, sluggish afternoons, eating tofu for lunch is a brilliant idea because it contains tyrosine—the amino acid that awakens the brain (it is also found in seafood and turkey). So, a salad with tofu and some leafy vegetables is the ideal lunch if you want to get some work done in the afternoons instead of dozing off.
- It packs a punch, with protein, iron, some omega-3 fatty acids, calcium and has some vitamin D too.
- It also delivers a lot of the mineral magnesium, which helps relieve stress and keeps our heart healthy.
- It contains some zinc, which is usually hard to find in foods and plays a big role in boosting our immunity.

CHANGE HOW YOU COOK TOFU

Here are a few delicious tofu recipes that are also easy to cook.

Sesame Tofu, 2 Ways

- **Sesame-crusted tofu:** Mix 3–4 tbsp maida, salt, pepper, choice of herbs to taste and 3–4 tbsp water in 1 bowl. In another bowl, mix 3–4 tbsp each of sesame seeds and breadcrumbs. Coat 200 gm of tofu chunks in the flour mix and then the sesame seeds and breadcrumbs. Bake at 180 °C for about 35–40 minutes, turning the pieces over after half the time. Enjoy!
- **Sesame-tofu stir-fry:** Lightly coat 200 gm tofu with some cornflour. In a bowl, combine 1 tbsp peanuts, 1 tbsp sesame seeds, some sliced ginger and 1 red pepper. Toss the tofu in gently. Heat 2 tbsp oil, add the tofu mixture and stir-fry until the sesame seeds are toasted and the tofu begins to brown. Remove the tofu and set it aside. In the same pan, add 250 gm of any mixed vegetables and sauté for 2–3 minutes. Add a sauce of your choice cook and stir gently until the mixture starts bubbling. Toss the tofu back into the pan, heat through and garnish with some more peanuts. Serve with rice.

Creamy Grilled Tofu

Evenly cube 200 gm tofu, 1 tomato and ½ a green pepper. Mix 3 tbsp hung curd, a few chopped cloves of garlic and chilli flakes, salt and pepper to taste. Marinate tofu and vegetables in the mixture and set it aside for 30 minutes. Grill the marinated tofu and vegetables in an oven (or pan-fry them) and eat with coriander–mint chutney.

Tofu Smoothie

Add ½ a cup of soft tofu, 1 cup of soy or almond milk, 1 chopped frozen banana and 1 tsp peanut butter in a mixer and blend for about 1 minute until smooth. Enjoy!

Spinach Tofu

Blanch 200 gm chopped spinach in some water. Let it cool. Remove the excess water and set it aside. Blend the spinach into a semi-soft paste and then pour the water we had kept aside into it. In a pan, sauté a pinch of cinnamon, 2–3 chopped garlic cloves and 1 inch ginger, 2 sliced green chillies and 1 finely chopped onion in 1 tbsp oil until the onion turns pink. Then, add 1 chopped tomato and sauté for a few minutes. Add the spinach, cover and cook for 10 minutes. Finally, add 200 gm cubed tofu pieces, a tbsp of cream and cook for 5 minutes on sim before serving.

Tofu and Amaranth Buddha Bowl

Stir-fry 50 gm amaranth with 200 gm vegetables of your choice in 1 tbsp of oil. Add 200 gm pan-fried, cubed tofu to the vegetables. Drizzle tahini on top. Dig in.

Tofu in Tomato Sauce

Heat 1 tbsp oil in a pan, add a pinch of cinnamon, some finely chopped ginger and garlic and a roughly chopped tomato. Cover and cook. When the tomatoes are soft and mushy, add some fresh basil leaves, herbs of your choice, salt and pepper to taste. Take the tomato sauce off the heat, add 200 gm pan-fried tofu to it. Pair this with a crisp toast.

Tofu Pasta

Heat 1 tbsp oil and sauté finely chopped garlic and a total of 200 gm of sliced mushrooms, baby corn, broccoli and French beans. Add 2 tbsp of any sauce (oyster, chilli tomato, peri peri, hoisin, etc.) and some water to the dish. Cover and cook for 6–7 minutes or till the vegetables are tender (but still crunchy). Add 200 gm cooked pasta and 200 gm pan-fried, cubed tofu before digging in.

Tofu Salad

Mix 2 tbsp light mayonnaise, 1 tbsp honey, a pinch of mustard powder and salt and pepper to taste. Add 2 chopped spring onions, some celery, a few chopped cloves of garlic and 100 gm pan-fried and cubed firm silken tofu to the mixture. Refrigerate for an hour, then dig in.

Tofu Biryani

Marinate 100 gm large tofu cubes for 15 minutes in 2 tbsp curd, ¼ tsp turmeric, 1 tsp *kewra* water (screw pine essence), green chillies, dry red chillies, ginger garlic paste, coriander leaves, mint leaves, sliced onions, salt, red chilli powder, coriander powder, roasted cumin powder and whole garam masalas (optional). Heat butter in a pressure cooker, cook the marinated tofu for 5 minutes, add 300 gm rice that has been soaked overnight. Pour water (1.5 cups of water for 1 cup of rice) and cook for 2 whistles. Let the pressure release and serve with pineapple raita.

Tofu Fusion

Heat 1 tbsp coconut oil in a pan, add a pinch each of mustard seeds, methi seeds, a few curry leaves and 2 whole dry red chillies. After they splutter, add 200 gm cubed firm tofu and sauté lightly. Season with salt to taste and some sambar powder. Cook for 5 minutes or until the tofu soaks up all the flavours. Dig in!

Tofu Nuggets

Whisk together ⅓ cup of soy milk, 1 tbsp mustard paste and salt and pepper to taste in a bowl. Place 1 cup of breadcrumbs in a separate bowl. Take 1 block of firm or extra-firm tofu and slice it lengthwise. Dip each piece of tofu in the soy milk mixture first and coat it with breadcrumbs after. Place the coated tofu pieces on a baking sheet and bake at 175 °C for 25 minutes, turning them once, until golden brown. Serve hot.

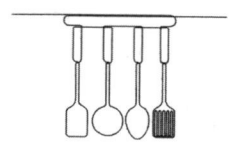

FOURTEEN

Tiny Fish, Big Benefits

The debate about whether a vegetarian or non-vegetarian diet is healthier for us is age-old. There is no straight answer to this question because there is no one correct way of eating. Everyone needs to find their own balance and stick to it. I believe that including some seafood in one's diet (being a pescatarian) is a good way to find the right balance of nutrition and ensure a good protein intake.

THE BENEFITS OF FISH

There are immense benefits to eating fish. I've listed some of them below.

- Besides getting good quality protein, it is now getting clear that being a pescatarian can help plump up the skin, smooth away wrinkles and reduce signs of ageing.
- Fish also provide the necessary essential fatty acids and other nutrients to keep our brain buzzing, boost our IQ (intelligence quotient) level and eyesight and even keep our memory sharp.
- Eating fish can reduce the risk of heart disease and help keep us calm.
- It can help reduce inflammation and joint pain too.

CHANGE HOW YOU COOK FISH

Here are a few delicious fish recipes that are also easy to cook.

Tuna Sandwich

Add 100 gm tuna and 1 tbsp garlic mayonnaise to a bowl and mash with a fork until a smooth paste forms. Add a few gherkins and Tabasco sauce to taste. Place a lettuce leaf on a slice of bread and top it with a large dollop of this mixture. Add a second slice on top and enjoy!

Mexican Sole

Heat 1 tbsp olive oil in a pan and sauté 2–3 chopped garlic cloves and 1 tbsp of chopped onion in it. Add 200 gm diced sole fish and cook for 5 minutes. Then, stir-fry 50 gm corn kernels, 1 diced tomato and 50 gm steamed beans in the pan. Add some stock or a splash of water, if required, before tossing in 100 gm diced bell peppers. Simmer for 5 minutes till the fish is cooked. Add salt, pepper and herbs to taste. Serve hot with steamed rice on the side.

Tuna Salad, 3 Ways

- **Tuna egg salad:** In a large bowl, mix ½ a red onion, ½ an avocado, ½ a cucumber, a few cherry tomatoes, 100 gm tuna and 1 hard-boiled egg, chopped. Season with 1 tbsp olive oil, salt, pepper and chilli flakes. Toss it all together, chill and dig in.
- **Tuna, white beans and spinach salad:** Combine 2 cups of spinach, 100 gm chunky tuna, ¾ cup of boiled lobia or white beans and ¾ cup of vegetables of your choice (try cucumbers and tomatoes) and top it with 1 tbsp each of balsamic vinegar and olive oil. Your salad is ready!
- **Tuna fruit salad:** In a bowl, mix 100 gm tuna, 1 chopped

apple (or pear) and 200 gm crudites (cucumbers, carrots, grapes, radish, *singhara* [water chestnuts]). Lightly season with salt, pepper, herbs to taste and top the salad off with some roasted *makhanas* (fox nuts) for crunch.

Baked Fish with Spinach

Sprinkle salt and lemon juice on 250 gm of sole fish and set aside. Take 1 tbsp oil in a pan and sauté 1 chopped onion, 2 minced garlic cloves, 1 chopped tomato, 1 tbsp dried parsley, salt and pepper to taste in it for 10 minutes. Spread this mixture in a baking dish, place the fish on top and arrange 100 gm fresh spinach, chopped and blanched, around it. Pour 1 tbsp wine (optional) over it. Cover with aluminium foil and bake in in an oven preheated to 350 °C for 30 minutes. Uncover and continue baking for 15 more minutes. Serve hot.

Coconut and Dhania Sole

Preheat the grill to 200 °C. To make the marinade, grind 1 red chilli with 2 cloves of garlic, 2 chopped spring onions, 1 tsp sugar, 50 ml coconut milk, a pinch of turmeric and some fresh coriander leaves and salt to taste to a smooth consistency. In an approximately 200 gm sole fillet, make two shallow cuts and place it on a baking sheet. Then, spoon half the marinade over the top. Grill for 3–4 minutes. Turn the sole over, spread the remaining marinade evenly on top and cook for another 3–4 minutes. Pair it with stir-fried mixed vegetables and dig in.

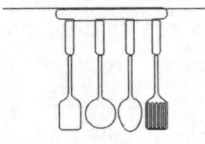

FIFTEEN

The Dynamite Chicken

Eating chicken has many benefits, some of which have been listed below.

- Chicken soup has proven recuperative powers, and chicken, particularly, is a brilliant way to add more protein, a nutrient most of us are short of, to our diets.
- It doesn't contain much fat, especially if you eat lean cuts.
- It also delivers multiple nutrients like vitamin B_{12}, tryptophan, iron, zinc, copper, choline and more.

∞

STORY TIME

Kiran Manral, an author, shared a very special memory related to chicken. She remembered that though she hadn't been a sickly child, she would often get feverish, especially during the monsoon, when she would get drenched coming home from school, or she would inevitably pick up some stomach bug from eating street food. Her mother believed that we need to drink something hot to beat the fever. So, she would make a lightly spiced chicken broth for young Kiran, with bread croutons. Kiran had to have a bowlful of it every night when she was ill. 'It's just chicken boiled in water with some sliced onions, a few pods of garlic, pepper, salt and a little chopped coriander on top to garnish with the croutons. I've tried to make chicken broth with bread croutons since, but it never tastes the same. Perhaps it was really that elusive *maa ke haath ka* taste,' Manral said. 'I remember as I got better, she would add shredded chicken into the soup. I don't know if it really aided my recovery, but I have great faith in its recuperative powers when I'm ill. Perhaps it is psychological,' she added.

CHANGE HOW YOU COOK CHICKEN

Here are a few delicious chicken recipes that are also easy to cook.

Chicken Wrap with Mango Mayonnaise

Combine 1 tbsp mayonnaise, ½ finely peeled mango and ¼ ground red pepper in a medium bowl. Add 100 gm chopped cooked chicken (leftovers will work just fine) and ½ chopped onion; stir to combine. Divide the chicken mixture evenly on top of flatbreads, spreading to cover half of each. Top the chicken mixture with a lettuce leaf. Roll it all up and enjoy!

Chicken in Wine

Marinate 250 gm chicken in 50 ml wine (red or white, whatever you prefer), 1 tbsp mustard sauce, 2 tbsp garlic paste, a dash of Tabasco sauce, rings of ½ an onion, slivers of ½ a green capsicum, 1 thinly sliced boiled potato and salt to taste for 2 hours. Heat 1 tbsp oil in a pan, pour everything we had marinated earlier in, cover and cook till the chicken is tender, turning the pieces over from time-to-time. Add a splash of water, if needed, before serving.

Chicken Salad, 4 Ways

- **Quick chicken salad**: In medium bowl, combine 100 gm cooked (boiled or roasted or pan-fried) chicken breast cubes, 1 chopped red bell pepper, a few torn lettuce leaves and 50 gm of any hard cheese, like Parmesan or cheddar. Toss in 1 tbsp mayonnaise, 2 tbsp milk, salt and white pepper and mix until the sauce properly coats the mixture. Cover and chill. To serve, place some greens on the dinner plate, and top them with the chicken mixture. Peel, core and finely chop 1 pear and sprinkle over the salad.
- **Tandoori-flavoured chicken salad**: Make diagonal slits in 300 gm boneless chicken and marinate it in 100 gm curd, 1 tbsp ginger garlic paste, 1 tsp ground red or green chillies, 1 tbsp tandoori chicken masala and salt to taste for at least 30 minutes or up to 2 hours. Pan-fry the chicken till it is well-browned and set aside. Toss 100 gm mixed lettuce, 50 gm feta and 50 gm cherry tomatoes with 1 tbsp olive oil and lay on the salad plate. Slice the pan-fried chicken and place it over the greens. To make the dressing, combine 1 tbsp olive oil, ½ tbsp vinegar and ½ tbsp honey. Drizzle this on top and serve.
- **Healthy chicken salad**: Boil 300 gm chicken with 1 bay leaf, 2 cloves, a bit of cinnamon and 2 black peppercorns in a pressure cooker till the chicken is cooked through. Debone and shred it. In a bowl, mix the shredded chicken with 1 chopped boiled potato, ½ sliced capsicum, 2 chopped green chillies, a bit of shredded cabbage and 2 tbsp lime juice. Garnish with a few walnuts and some cubed pineapples before serving.
- **Chicken fajita salad:** Marinate 100 gm boneless chicken in 1 tbsp oil, 2 tbsp lemon juice, 2 cloves of garlic, ½ tsp cumin powder and ½ tsp oregano. Sauté 1 chopped onion for 2 minutes. Separate the chicken and the marinade, setting the latter aside. Stir-fry the chicken in the pan until it begins

to brown. Add ½ chopped red pepper, 2 chopped chillies and the marinade into the pan. Cook for 2 minutes. Stir in 10 almonds. Serve atop shredded lettuce and cubed tomatoes.

Chicken Tikka

In a large mixing bowl, combine 300 gm of cubed boneless chicken with 1 tbsp lime juice, 1 tbsp garlic paste, 2 tbsp curd, parsley, pepper, salt and red chilli powder to taste. Rub the marinade well into the chicken pieces; cover and refrigerate for a few hours. Place on a well-greased grilling pan and grill the chicken at 160 °C for about an hour, till it's cooked through.

Basic Green Chicken

Heat 1 tbsp ghee, add ½ tsp cumin seeds, ½ inch grated ginger, 2–3 cloves of garlic and cook for 2 minutes. Stir in 250 gm of boiled and blended spinach. Add 300 gm boneless chicken, 1 chopped tomato, some fresh coriander and some water. Add salt to taste, cover and cook (or pressure cook) till the chicken is done before serving.

Steamed Chicken

Mix 2 finely chopped spring onions, some grated ginger, 1 tbsp rice vinegar, 1 tbsp soy sauce, salt and black pepper to taste. Rub this marinade on a 200–300 gm chicken breast and let it marinate for 2 hours. Place the chicken in a steamer for 30 minutes. Add some greens (spinach, bok choy, etc.) and steam for 5 more minutes. Pair with a spicy dip and enjoy.

Sweet Stir-Fried Chicken

Heat oil in a pan and cook 250 gm boneless chicken in it, until it is lightly brown. Stir-fry 1 tbsp minced garlic and ginger, 1 sliced onion, 50 gm peas, 1 chopped carrot, 50 gm broccoli and

½ a bell pepper until crisp yet tender. Add 100 gm of pineapple chunks and stir until heated through.

Whisk ½ cup chicken broth, 2 tbsp soy sauce, 1 tbsp pineapple juice (optional), 1 tbsp brown sugar and 1 tbsp cornflour together. Pour this over the chicken and vegetable mixture, stirring continuously until it thickens. Pair with brown rice.

Quick Chicken Breast

Cut 250 gm chicken breast into small pieces. Heat 1 tbsp oil in pan, shallow-fry the chicken until cooked thoroughly. Add salt and pepper to taste. Place some rocket leaves and pomegranate in a bowl, toss in 1 tbsp olive oil, chicken, salt, pepper and some mustard paste to taste. Dig in!

Caramelized Lemon Chicken

Season a 300 gm chicken breast with 1 tbsp lemon juice, 1 tbsp olive oil and salt to taste. Preheat the grill to 160 °C. Place the chicken on a baking sheet and sprinkle some sugar on it. Grill for 3–4 minutes until caramelized. Turn the chicken over, sprinkle some more sugar on the other side and grill until the chicken is cooked through and golden for about 1 hour. Serve hot.

Chicken with Mushrooms

In a pan with heated oil, sauté chopped garlic, sliced onion, sliced mushrooms and puréed tomatoes. Add boneless chicken strips and season with salt, pepper and herbs of your choice to taste. Pour some water over the chicken, cover and cook on a low flame till the chicken is done. Add a few strips of capsicum and cook for another minute before serving.

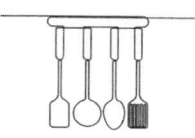

SIXTEEN

Chill with Curd

I really don't need to convince anyone to like curd anymore—everyone already knows how healthy this humble food really is. It has been a constant presence in most Indian cuisines in some form or the other. Most of us have grown up eating raita at least once a day because not only does it make a perfect accompaniment to meals that we Indians have but also because, traditionally, it is believed to be a digestive and a gut strengthener.

STORY TIME

Manish Mehrotra, a celebrity chef, said that curd is an important part of not just our food but also our culture. 'It is considered as one of the purest forms of food that is offered to the gods—*charnamrut* is made with it, and the statues of gods are bathed in it. Whether it is East, West, North or South India, curd plays an important part in our day-to-day meal plans, and raita, I feel, is a recipe that makes the slightly bland, boring curd more interesting and exciting. That is why there is no end to the type of raitas you can make. In fact, there are a thousand types of raitas that can be made and the innovation with raitas is totally up to a person. Sky's the limit,' he shared. Chef Mehrotra's favourite raita is *boondi* raita, as he feels that it has an interesting texture. He feels that the silky smoothness of the curd and its savoury flavour complements Indian meals.

∽

THE BENEFITS OF CURD

Some of the many benefits of eating curd have been listed below.

- It is packed with calcium, magnesium, vitamin B and good bacteria. This high-protein food strengthens immunity, lowers blood pressure and is low on calories.
- It can alter moods in a good way and boost our brain function.
- The protein in curd is easily digestible, yes, even by those who are lactose intolerant. So, it is a great way to add some good calcium and protein to your diet.
- It can help us remain alert and curb the stresses of life because it contains the amino acid tyrosine, which is needed for the production of the neurotransmitters dopamine and noradrenalin, which help with better learning and memory. Now you know the logic behind eating dahi cheeni before exams.
- Finally, curd is versatile enough to be eaten as a snack or as part of a main meal, at work or on the go and in sweet or savoury forms.

CHANGE HOW YOU COOK WITH CURD

We all know curd tastes great. However, what I want to talk about here is how to make this already 'good' food even 'better' by pairing it with the right additions.

Here are a few delicious curd recipes that are also easy to cook.

Banana, Pomegranate and Flaxseeds Raita

In a bowl, whisk some curd. To it, add 1 chopped banana, some pomegranate seeds and 1 tsp of honey. Sprinkle 1 tbsp roasted flaxseeds on top and serve.

Note: Curd delivers good bacteria (called probiotics). So, it is a great gut food. Both flaxseeds and bananas deliver prebiotics as well, which help the curd's healthy bacteria grow. Pomegranate is also a good gut food.

Bitter Gourd Raita

Rub salt over 100 gm of thinly sliced bitter gourd (*karela*). After some time, rinse the slices and fry them in some mustard oil and set aside. In a bowl, beat 250 gm curd, 2 chopped green chillies and salt to taste. To this mixture, add the cooked bitter gourd slices. Next, add 1 chopped onion, either raw if you like the crunch or slightly seared and softened in a little oil with mustard seeds.

Note: If you cannot stomach bitter gourd, try this raita. It is delicious and also a perfect dish to introduce this vegetable to your diet.

Bhindi Raita

Stir-fry 50 gm chopped bhindi (okra) in a little mustard oil till it is crisp. Whisk some curd and season it with roasted cumin seeds and black salt. Add the fried bhindi to the curd. Temper mustard seeds, cumin seeds, curry leaves, peanuts, chopped green chillies and ginger (you can add some sliced onions too) and pour this tadka over the raita.

Note: Bhindi contains fibre that helps the gut function better and prevents constipation, bloating, cramping and excess gas. So, curd and okra together are pure magic for solving gut issues.

Spinach Raita

Boil 100 gm spinach for 1 minute uncovered (to leech out the oxalic acid it contains, which interferes with the absorption of some nutrients) and chop it finely with kitchen scissors. Alternatively, temper some cumin seeds in a little oil, add chopped spinach and sauté on high heat until it is tender and most of the water has evaporated. Add the cooked spinach to a bowl of thick curd. Set it aside. Make a tempering with a pinch of mustard seeds, a little urad dal and 2 chopped green or red chillies in 1 tsp mustard oil. Add the tadka, salt to taste and a little bit of grated *amla* (Indian gooseberry) to the raita. Chill and serve.

Note: Curd contains bone-friendly calcium and spinach has other nutrients that are good for bone health, like magnesium, and it is also a rich source of vitamin K. So, this combination is great for maintaining bone health.

Flaxseed and Bottle Gourd Raita

Combine ½ a thickly grated bottle gourd with 1 cup of water. Cover and cook on a medium flame till it's cooked through. Cool and add 1 cup of beaten curd to it. Season with a few mint leaves, ½ tsp roasted cumin seeds, 1 tbsp roasted and coarsely ground flaxseeds and black salt to taste. Mix well. Refrigerate for at least 1 hour and serve chilled.

Note: Not only do flaxseeds add crunch but also contain omega-3 fatty acids and prebiotics. Bottle gourd is a quintessential summer vegetable that delivers lots of water (it is 96 per cent water). It is inherently cooling and loaded with potassium, which helps keep the blood pressure down and maintains the electrolyte balance in our bodies. Thus, this is a delicious and super healthy combination.

Beetroot Raita

Boil and grate 1 beetroot. Heat 1 tsp oil, add 1 chopped green chilli, a pinch of black mustard seeds, 1 dry red chilli, some grated ginger and the grated beetroot to it and cook for 2 minutes. Add the mixture to 1 cup of beaten curd, add salt and roasted cumin powder to taste and serve.

Note: Curd is known to help calm us down and make us happy. Betaine, which is used in some depression medications, and tryptophan in beetroot help us relax. So, this one this is a potent, feel-good raita.

Roasted Almond Raita

Beat 1 cup of yoghurt, add 6–7 chopped roasted almonds, some vanilla essence and spice it up with some cinnamon, cardamom or ginger. Dig in!

Note: Ever wonder why milk is D-fortified? Your body needs vitamin D, which is generally difficult to find, to better absorb the bone-building calcium found in milk. Almond is one of the rare food sources of vitamin D (among other nutrients). So, almonds help put the calcium in curd to good use. And the fat in curd returns the favour by improving the absorption of the fat-soluble vitamin D in almonds.

Cucumber Raita

Whisk together 1 cup of grated cucumber, 1 cup of curd, 1 tbsp fresh mint or coriander leaves, 2 tbsp lemon juice and 2 crushed garlic cloves. Refrigerate for 1 hour before digging in.

Note: This raita is refreshing, light on the stomach, immunity boosting, delicious and a hydrating combination for the body that prevents dehydration.

Fresh Fruit Raita

Throw several types of fresh fruits, like apples, grapes and mango in a blender and blitz them at low speed till they partly liquefied. Add yoghurt and a pinch of brown sugar to it. Refrigerate and serve cool.

Note: It is the easiest way to add in more fruits to your diet. Fruits have essential fibre and the protein in the curd helps slow down the insulin response to the sugar from the fruits in the body. This raita can also help tame sweet cravings while delivering antioxidants aplenty.

Banana Raita

Slice a banana or mash it roughly with a fork and set it aside. Whisk 1 cup of curd, add 1 tsp sugar and a pinch of salt (it helps enhance the sweetness) and pour it over the banana. In a pan, heat ½ tsp coconut oil and add a pinch each of mustard seeds, urad dal and a few curry leaves to it. Pour this tempering over the banana curd mix. Grate some coconut shavings (fresh or dried) over this mixture. Stir well, chill and dig in.

CHEF MANISH MEHROTRA'S FAVOURITE RAITAS

It is difficult to be unimaginative with raita, as it is a versatile dish. Celebrity chef Manish Mehrotra, from Indian Accent, The Manor, New Delhi, agreed with me. 'Most vegetables and spices pair well with curd, so multiple combinations and interesting customizations are possible,' he said. Here are some of Chef Mehrotra's favourite raitas:

Pears and Masala Amla Raita

Ingredients: 250 gm curd, 70 gm diced pears, 1 tbsp chopped masala amla, 2 tsp salt, 1 tsp crushed and roasted cumin seeds

Method: In a mixing bowl, add the curd, salt and cumin seeds and mix using a whisk. Add the diced pears and half of the masala amla. Adjust the seasoning according to taste. Refrigerate and serve cold, garnished with the remaining amla.

Beetroot and Goat Cheese Raita

Ingredients: 250 gm curd, ¼ cup (50 gm) goat cheese, 40 gm beetroot, 2 tsp salt, 1 tsp crushed roasted cumin seeds, 4 tbsp olive oil, 1 tsp chaat masala, 1 lemon

Method: Take the beetroot, apply olive oil and salt to it. Wrap it in aluminium foil and roast in a preheated oven for 20 minutes at 180 °C. Let it cool.

Peel and dice the beetroot. Marinate it in olive oil, chaat masala and lemon juice. In a mixing bowl, add curd along with goat cheese, salt and cumin seeds. Mix them thoroughly using a whisk. Adjust the seasoning according to taste. Refrigerate and serve cold, garnished with the diced beetroot.

Wild Rice and Cucumber Raita

Ingredients: 250 gm curd, 30 gm boiled wild rice/quinoa/ any other whole grain, 20 gm seedless cucumber, 2 tsp salt, 4 tbsp oil, 1 tsp urad dal, 1 tsp mustard seeds

Method: Dice the cucumber into small pieces. Take a pan and put it on a flame, add oil and heat it up. Add mustard seeds and urad dal and sauté them, then add curry leaves. Remove this tadka from pan and place it on a kitchen towel to remove excess oil. In a mixing bowl, add curd along with salt and cumin seeds and mix thoroughly. Add the boiled wild rice and diced cucumber. Adjust the seasoning according to taste and top it with the prepared tadka. Refrigerate and serve cold, garnished with fried curry leaves.

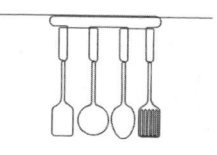

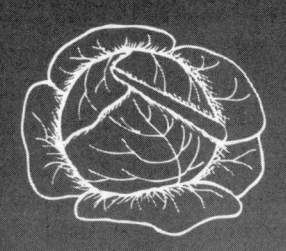

PART 4

The Vegetable Rack

If I had to pick the one habit I wish I could help people develop, it would have to be eating more vegetables. And by this, I don't mean eating just the vegetables that you like or can tolerate but learning to eat a whole variety of them.

So, stop thinking about vegetables as a side dish. In fact, your focus should be on eating a substantial number of vegetables in every meal. This is imperative to meet your ideal daily nutritional quota.

To make vegetables more exciting, it helps to change the way you cook. For example, when making pasta, poha, upma, khichdi, daliya, etc., make sure that the vegetables to carbohydrates ratio is 1:1, eventually building it up to 2:1. By just making this one change in your approach to food, you can make your meals healthier, tastier and much more interesting.

Also having a variety of vegetable is the most important diktat here, as all of them have something going for them. So, make a list and incorporate one new vegetable in your diet every week. Give it a fair shot. Cook it in at least 3-4 ways and then decide which one works for you. Think of the way our mothers made us try new foods and try to replicate them. Trust me, you will be surprised.

Let me tell you a story. A friend of mine hated tomatoes all her life. But, one day, when she was sitting with me, she ate a plateful of fresh, raw tomato slices, doused in balsamic vinegar and seasoned with just a few basil leaves, pine nuts and some herbs. 'Delicious!' she declared. She went back home and called me, telling me that she regretted that it had taken her 3 decades to discover the delight of this ubiquitous vegetable. Now, she is working on developing a taste for mushrooms.

So, I suggest you too start trying vegetables you have resisted eating so far. Slowly, with trial and error, you will have a far more extensive repertoire of vegetables to choose from and eat. And your body will show its appreciation by keeping you safe from chronic non-communicable diseases, like diabetes, heart disease, and so on.

SEVENTEEN

The Many Ways to Eat Beetroot

After you read the many benefits of beetroot, you won't be able to ignore it. Besides, this red beauty is one root that you can easily stock up on, as it doesn't spoil that quickly.

STORY TIME

Manish Mehrotra, a celebrity chef, really likes beetroot. He shares that as a child, he somehow never ate much beetroot, but he actually has a very bad memory of it from his college years. 'We were often served a beetroot salad, which was really horrible, and we were not allowed to waste any food. One day, by mistake, I don't know how, I took a lot of that salad on my plate and that day was one of the worst days of my life. Since we were not allowed to throw any food in the mess, I had to fill my mouth with that horrible salad that I hated and then run to the hostel to just throw it away in the dustbin. After that day, I just stopped eating beetroot completely. But, slowly, when I started travelling abroad and started eating in different restaurants, I started liking it again, and now beetroot is always on my menu,' he shared.

THE BENEFITS OF BEETROOT

Eating beetroot has many benefits. Some of them have been listed below.

- Beetroot is low in calories (200 gm contains only 85 calories).
- It is loaded with fibre (200 gm contains almost 6 gm fibre).
- It contains betaine (used in some depression medications) and tryptophan, which help us relax and make us feel happier. So, it is kind of like chocolate but without the fat. Betaines can also help eliminate toxins and cleanse our body.
- The betaine in beetroot gives it a deep red colour (that is why it is best to buy the deepest red beetroot you can) and helps the body fight against free radicals—the harbingers of a myriad lifestyle diseases and accelerated ageing.

CHANGE HOW YOU COOK BEETROOT

Considering its many benefits, you want beetroot to be on your menu. If you just don't know how to eat it (besides just slicing and eating it as a salad), here are a few delicious beetroot recipes that are also easy to cook.

Jazzy Juice

Do you find the plain beetroot juice a little uninteresting? You can just grate some orange peel or lemon peel in it. Do you prefer savoury things? You can spice up beetroot juice with fresh ginger or hot peppers too.

Beetroot Buttermilk

Purée 1 boiled beetroot in a mixer. To it, add 1 cup of curd with 1 cup of water and whisk it together. Next, heat ½ tsp oil, add ¼ tsp mustard seeds, 5–6 curry leaves, ½ tsp ginger and 1 green chilli chopped finely. Add the tempering to the beetroot buttermilk. Chill and serve.

Beetroot Cake

Peel 1 large beetroot and 1 small potato and grate them. Season with salt and pepper, add 1 egg white (or half-soaked bread or bread crumbs) and 2–3 sliced almonds to it. Grease a non-stick pan with very little oil, place the potato and beet mixture into it in a thin layer, and press down a bit. Cook until it is golden brown on one side, then carefully flip to cook on the other side. Serve hot.

Beetroot Chicken Salad

Marinate 2 steamed beetroots in 1 tbsp fresh lemon juice, 1 tsp olive oil and fresh herbs of your choice to taste. Place in a roasting tin and roast for 40 minutes at 200 °C. Peel, chop and toss into a salad with 50 gm of chopped and cooked (pan-fried or roasted or boiled) chicken breast, a few walnuts, raisins and 1 tbsp olive oil.

Dressed Beetroots

Chill 100 gm of boiled and cubed beetroot. Mix 2 tbsp orange juice, 1 tbsp olive oil, a pinch each of salt, black pepper, mustard powder and orange zest in a bowl and whisk well. Pour the dressing over the beetroot pieces and garnish with spring onion and mint. Serve chilled.

Beetroot Thoran

In 1 tsp coconut oil, temper 1 tsp mustard seeds, 1 tsp urad dal, a few curry leaves and a couple of red chillies. Add grated beetroot and season with salt to taste. Stir-fry till the beetroot is cooked. Garnish with freshly grated coconut or dried coconut flakes. Mix and eat with appam or paratha.

Boiled Beetroot Salad with Berries and Garden Greens

Place 30 gm thinly sliced beetroot on a plate. In a separate bowl, mix 40 gm salad leaves, 5 gm capers or gherkins, 5–6 strawberries, 8 ml olive oil and salt and pepper to taste. Layer this salad on top of the thinly sliced beetroot. Crumble 15 gm goat cheese on top of the salad. Serve cold. Pair with any bread.

⁂

CHEF MANISH MEHROTRA'S BEETROOT TIKKI AND GREEN BEANS FOOGATH

Beetroot Tikki

Ingredients: 1 beetroot, 15 ml ghee, 1 gm each of finely chopped ginger, garlic and green chilli, 1 gm red chilli powder, salt to taste, 1 gm coriander powder, 10 gm boiled potatoes (peeled and grated), 5 gm crushed walnuts, 2 gm chaat masala, 1 gm garam masala, a few chopped coriander leaves, 15 gm tempura flour, 10 gm panko breadcrumbs

Method: Wash the beetroot and boil in water till it is about 80 per cent cooked. Drain and allow to cool. Peel and finely grate it. Heat ghee in a pan. Add garlic, green chillies, ginger and beetroot and sauté. Season with salt, red chilli powder and coriander powder. Sauté till the moisture evaporates. Add chaat masala and boiled potatoes. Continue to sauté for a while. Garnish with garam masala, coriander leaves and crushed walnuts. Allow the mixture to cool and form small tikkis.

Make a tempura batter by dissolving ice cold water in the

tempura flour. Put a little batter on the top and bottom of the tikkis using your fingers and coat with panko breadcrumbs. Shallow-fry the tikkis in ghee till they are golden brown on both sides.

Green Beans Foogath

Ingredients: 10 green beans, 5 ml ghee, 2 gm mustard seeds, 3 gm urad dal, a few curry leaves, 1 gm finely chopped ginger, salt to taste, 5 gm grated coconut, 1 gm chopped coriander leaves

Method: Blanch the beans in salted boiling water for a minute and shock them in ice cold water. Drain. Heat ghee in a pan. Add mustard seeds and allow them to crackle. Add urad dal and sauté till it is golden. Add curry leaves, ginger, beans and sauté. Add salt and finish with chopped coriander and grated coconut.

Wasabi Dressing

Ingredients: 20 ml hung curd, 2 gm wasabi paste, 3 ml coriander chutney, 1 gm each of finely chopped ginger, garlic, green chillies, coriander leaves, 2 gm chaat masala, salt to taste, 3 ml lemon juice, roasted walnuts and micro greens for garnish

Method: Mix hung curd with wasabi, chutney, ginger, garlic, green chillies, salt, chaat masala, coriander leaves and lemon juice. Set the mixture aside for a while and strain.

Pipe wasabi dressing on top of the beetroot tikkis and serve foogath on the side. Garnish with walnuts and greens.

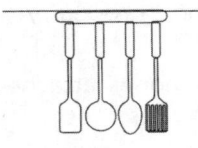

EIGHTEEN

Cauliflower Calling

Cauliflower, being commonplace, used to not be taken seriously. But then came the lockdown and people realized that this easily available cruciferous vegetable lasts for a long time without spoiling and is dependable. So, they began looking at it from a new perspective and it finally started getting the respect it deserves.

∽

STORY TIME

Bhavana Reddy, a Kuchipudi dancer, has always loved cauliflower, even when it was considered rather blah by most of her friends.

'My favourite recipe is *neela gobi koora*, which literally translates to watery cauliflower sabzi. It is something like a cauliflower stew that I simply go nuts over. In fact, even as I am writing this to you on a Tuesday, the day I only eat vegetarian food, my mouth is watering because neela gobi koora is a dish my mom would cook very often on vegetarian days. For me, it was the irresistible substitute for mutton pulusu—a sort of mutton bone curry that she would make that I loved too.

'I have so many memories attached to this dish. Once,

mom had made it and my cousins were over. My cousin brother made a bet with me that he could eat more rotis than me and so the competition began. I beat him and ate 7 rotis for lunch, only because neela gobi koora had been made that day. This was when I was in my pre-teens.

Living in the USA, one day, I was craving this recipe. So much so, I ended up experimenting and if I my say so myself, I did a fine job of making it and satisfied my craving.'

Bhavana Reddy's Neela Gobi Koora

'In a pressure cooker, make the usual tadka with oil, ginger garlic paste, roughly grated onion, dhania powder and salt. Then, add cauliflower florets and some potato chunks to it. Add chopped tomatoes, red chilli powder, turmeric powder and finally some water, and let the pressure cooker work its magic. I usually add all this stuff approximately, so it is hard for me to mention the accurate measurements. And, of course, one must add fresh coriander leaves for garnish. It is a super simple recipe and tastes mind-blowing with roti. It is like a warm comfort food, but nice and spicy—Telugu style.'

∞

THE BENEFITS OF CAULIFLOWER

Eating cauliflower has many benefits, some of which have been listed below.

- It is an extremely low-calorie vegetable (1 cup or about 120 gm just has 25 calories), and it has some fibre too.
- It is an excellent source of vitamins (C, K, B vitamins) and minerals (potassium, manganese, magnesium,

phosphorus), containing trace amounts of almost all vitamins and minerals that you need.
- It is cancer-preventive, thanks to the presence of antioxidants, glucosinolates and isothiocyanates that help slow the growth of cancer cells.
- It has the ability to bind together with bile acids and helps regulate blood cholesterol levels.
- It is a rare food source of choline, which is important for brain development and a healthy nervous system.

CHANGE HOW YOU COOK CAULIFLOWER

Here are a few delicious cauliflower recipes that are also easy to cook.

Cauliflower Salad

Cut 1 head of a cauliflower into florets and pulse briefly in a food processor to make cauliflower rice and set it aside. Pulse soft spinach leaves in the food processor with 1 onion and the juice of 2 lemons to mix them well. Add salt and pepper to taste. Mix the cauliflower rice with the spinach and onion mix. Garnish with a few diced cherry tomatoes and mint leaves before serving.

Orange Cauliflower

Peel and segment 2 oranges and set them aside. Marinate 1 small cauliflower cut into florets and 1 quartered potato cut into cubes in a little turmeric and salt.

Heat 1 tbsp mustard oil, add the potato and cauliflower; gently sauté till they turn golden brown. Transfer the vegetables to a plate and set aside.

In 1 tbsp ghee in a pan, stir-fry 1 clove, 1 cardamom, ½ a bay leaf and a small piece of cinnamon for a few seconds. Add

1 tsp ginger paste, 1 tbsp onion paste, ½ tsp turmeric and 1 tsp red chilli powder. Sauté till the masala is cooked. Add the sautéed vegetables, some water and salt to taste; cover and simmer till they are tender. Stir in 1 sliced green chilli and half the orange segments. Simmer for another 4–5 minutes. Add 1 tsp sugar, remove from heat, decorate with the remaining orange segments and serve.

Cauliflower Samosa

Knead 100 gm whole wheat flour into a dough with water, salt, ½ tsp soda and 1 tbsp oil. Set it aside.

Heat 2 tbsp oil in pan, add a pinch each of methi seeds, *kalonji* (black caraway), mustard, fennel seeds (*saunf*) and cumin seeds. Then, add 1 small, grated cauliflower and 1 small finely chopped potato. Sprinkle salt to taste along with 1 tsp ginger paste and cook till it's done. Garnish with fresh coriander leaves, 1 chopped green chilli, 1 tbsp peanuts and a pinch of roasted cumin powder. Cook for 2 minutes, set it aside and let it cool.

Roll out the dough into small, thick puris and cut them into semi-circles. Roll into small cones and fill with the stuffing. Seal the open edges to form samosas. Deep-fry in mustard oil and eat them hot.

Cauliflower Mash

Separate 1 cauliflower head into florets and discard the core. Steam the florets till they are tender, add 2–3 tbsp milk, 2 tbsp butter, 2 tbsp sour cream, salt and pepper to taste, and mash until it is smooth. Serve as a side with eggs, chicken or fish.

Chilli Cauliflower

Marinate the florets of 1 medium-sized cauliflower in salt and red chilli powder for 30 minutes.

Whisk together ½ cup cornflour, ½ cup maida, 1 chopped green chilli, 1 tsp baking powder and ½ tsp salt in ½ cup of water till the batter reaches a consistency that can coat the cauliflower.

Squeeze the florets to remove excess water and toss them in the batter till they are well-coated. In a kadai, deep-fry the florets till they are golden brown and crisp. Set them aside.

In a separate pan, heat 1 tbsp oil and stir-fry 1 diced onion, 1 diced capsicum and 2 diced spring onions for 1 minute. Add 3 cups of water along with 1 tbsp soy sauce and 1 tbsp chilli sauce. Stir, bring to a boil and simmer for 3 minutes. Toss the fried cauliflower pieces in the sauce, garnish with chopped spring onions and serve hot.

Salad on a Stick

Make a dip by mixing ½ cup of plain curd, 2 tbsp oil, 2 tbsp honey, 1 tbsp white wine vinegar, 1.5 tsp mustard paste, salt and pepper to taste.

Skewer cherry tomatoes, cucumber, steamed cauliflower and cubed paneer, all cut into cubes on a toothpick. Arrange the sticks around the bowl of dressing, dip and enjoy.

Gobi Musallam

Dunk 1 whole cauliflower in warm salt water for 10 minutes, then set it aside. Meanwhile, blend 2 onions, a 2-inch piece of ginger, 8 garlic cloves and 3 tomatoes, salt to taste and add 1 tbsp of meat masala (or some chilli powder, coriander powder, garam masala and amchoor) to it.

Place the cauliflower in a pressure cooker, pour the sauce over it, drizzle 2 tbsp mustard oil on it and pressure cook for 1 whistle and then cook on sim for 3–4 minutes. Sprinkle cumin powder and coriander leaves on top. Enjoy with roti and raita.

Tandoori Cauliflower

Cut 500 gm cauliflower into medium-sized florets. Mix 1 tbsp ginger paste, 2 tsp garlic paste, ½ tsp ajwain powder, 2 tsp red chilli powder, 1 cup curd, 1 cup of besan (chickpea flour), 3 tbsp oil, salt to taste and marinate the florets for an hour. Preheat the oven, skewer the coated florets or place them on a plate and grill for 5 minutes on both sides. Serve with mint chutney.

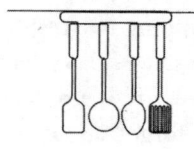

NINETEEN

Cool as a Cucumber

Remember the childhood days, when you would sit in the sun, reading and chomping on freshly cut cucumber sticks, seasoned with just black salt and lemon juice? They seemed heavenly then, but as we grew up, and cucumber became commonplace, we mostly forgot about it. Hardly anyone takes cucumber seriously now. It is always considered to be an accompaniment and never the star of any menu. In fact, it is often even bought as an afterthought. But things have changed lately because, during the lockdown, we realized that this vegetable was available in plenty and most of us did not know just what to do with it. After all, how many cucumbers can you add to the salad, right?

THE BENEFITS OF CUCUMBER

Cucumber is immensely beneficial to us. I have listed some of the benefits below.

- It keeps you hydrated and cool from the inside because it is mostly water.
- It is very low on calories (there are only 16 calories in an average-sized cucumber). So, eating it helps prevent weight gain.
- It is loaded with flavonoids that are antioxidants and

have anti-inflammatory properties, which are much needed to keep us safe from myriad infections.
- It has compounds called lignans and cucurbitacin, which have anti-cancer properties.
- It contains vitamin K, which is crucial for bone health.
- It also helps relieve constipation because it provides both fibre and water.
- It is a good source of fisetin, a flavonoid that helps improve memory and decreases the risk of Alzheimer's.
- It is rich in potassium and magnesium, which may help lower blood pressure.
- Finally, it is an extremely versatile ingredient that can work well as a light summer lunch, a drink, a soup and even a cooling salad.

CHANGE HOW YOU COOK CUCUMBER

Here are a few delicious cucumber recipes that are also easy to cook.

Cucumber Sticks

Cut cucumbers into sticks, sprinkle them with salt and pepper, refrigerate and munch on them all day.

Detox Water

Add slices of cucumber to room temperature water. Let it sit for a couple of hours and then serve.

Weight Loss Slush

Blend ½ cucumber, a small piece of grated ginger, 2 cloves of crushed garlic, a bit of fresh turmeric grated (or ½ tsp turmeric powder), a pinch of pepper, 10–12 stalks of coriander, a few mint leaves, 10 curry leaves, 1 grated amla and 1 tbsp chia or basil seeds (soaked in water for at least 20 minutes) with some cold water. Squeeze the juice of 1 lemon in the slush and serve chilled.

Cucumber Salad, 3 Ways

- **Peanut cucumber salad**: In a bowl, add 2 chopped cucumbers, 2 sliced green chillies, 2 tbsp roasted peanuts, 1 tbsp lemon juice and salt to taste. In a small, heated pan, add 1 tsp coconut oil, a pinch of mustard seeds, ½ tsp chana dal, 1 dry red chilli and 8–10 curry leaves. Add the tempering to the salad and garnish with freshly grated coconut (or dried coconut flakes) and coriander leaves. Toss and dig in.
- **Thai cucumber salad**: Combine 2 peeled and sliced cucumbers, ½ a cup of very finely minced spring onions, ½ cup of bean sprouts, ½ cup of finely sliced red or yellow capsicum, salt to taste, 2 tsp sugar and 2 tbsp vinegar. Mix gently. Cover tightly and let it marinate in the refrigerator for at least 4 hours. Garnish with fresh basil leaves and chopped red chillies before serving cold.
- **Maharashtrian cucumber salad (*khamang kakdi*)**: To 2 cut cucumbers, add 2 tbsp of fresh coconut, 2 tbsp of curd, some finely chopped coriander, ground black pepper and salt to taste. Make a tadka in ghee with a pinch each of cumin and mustard seeds and hing, 1 chopped green chilli and a few curry leaves. Top it off with roasted and crushed peanuts, mix and serve.

Cucumber Soup, 2 Ways

- **Cucumber and curd soup**: Blend 500 gm chopped cucumber, 1 cup of chopped mint leaves and some chopped garlic until smooth. Pour the cucumber mixture into a large bowl and whisk in 1.25 cups of plain non-fat curd, ½ tbsp fresh lemon

juice, 1 tsp sea salt and a pinch of freshly ground black pepper. Chill in the refrigerator for 2 hours and serve.
- **Chilled cucumber and tomato soup**: Deseed and finely chop 1 small cucumber and 1 small red bell pepper. Roast 1 large garlic clove and smash it. Reserve some of the cucumber and bell pepper and purée the rest with 2 cups of tomato juice and the roasted garlic. Stir in the rest of the cucumber and bell pepper. Season with salt, pepper, the juice of 1 lemon, a few chopped basil leaves, a few dashes of Tabasco sauce and a few dashes of Worcestershire sauce. Chill and enjoy.

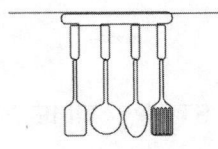

TWENTY

Relishing Bottle Gourd

If you too think of bottle gourd as a tasteless and watery vegetable, this chapter is for you. Instead of avoiding it, you just need to know how to make it more interesting.

∽

STORY TIME

Chef Kishi Arora, a TED fellow, chefpreneur and alumni of the Culinary Institute of America, loves bottle gourd. She even grows it in her terrace garden, just so that she can always have a fresh supply. 'I am diabetic but I like to eat a bit of meetha after my meals. So, my mom's lauki (bottle gourd) barfi works for me perfectly. I just love to have a small portion of this supremely healthy meetha every now and then,' she shared.

Chef Kishi Arora's Lauki ki Barfi

'Buy a fresh and tender bottle gourd that is firm and smooth. It can be any colour, from light green to dark green. My mom likes to buy the pale green, desi variety. Make sure it does not have bruises, cuts, blemishes or soft spots. If it is hard, it is likely to be old and stringy, which we don't want.

'Wash, dry peel and deseed about 500 gm of this freshly bought bottle gourd. From the thick side of the grater, grate the bottle gourd and squeeze out all the liquid. Heat 1–1.5 tbsp of ghee and cook the bottle gourd on a low flame. Meanwhile, dry roast some assorted nuts. My mother adds melon seeds because my dad used to love them, and she adds some raisins for me. You can also add pistachio or any nuts you like. Once the bottle gourd is partially cooked, add $1/2$ cup of sugar. My mother uses regular sugar, but you can add any kind of sugar.

'Once the gourd is cooked [there will be a *chashani*, or sugar syrup, in which it will get cooked] and dried out, add some of the roasted nuts. Next, add 1 cup of milk powder. You can alternatively add *khoya* [a kind of Indian dairy product]. Here, you can also add ¼ tsp cardamom powder (I don't like it but my mum does) and cook some more.

'In the end, pour it in a cake pan greased with some ghee. Garnish with the leftover dry fruits. Sometimes, my mother uses my edible cake colours and adds a drop of green colour to make the barfi "happier"! I don't fight with her; whatever brings a big smile on her face works for me. Let the barfi set for an hour. Finally, add some gold or silver foil on top and cut into desired shapes and sizes.

'Also, if everything is cooked correctly, you can store this barfi for 10 days. My mother stores it in a glass container, and I mostly have a piece after my meals. My mom also adds desiccated coconut along with the milk powder. She even made it with goji and cranberries once! I loved the cranberry version. For the perfect barfi, just make sure you patiently cook everything on a low flame.'

THE BENEFITS OF BOTTLE GOURD

Eating bottle gourd has immense benefits. Some of them have been listed below.

- This underrated vegetable is available during the hotter months, when it can act as a natural coolant. Not many know that this quintessential summer vegetable is extremely hydrating (it is 96 per cent water), inherently cooling and keeps the body cool and refreshed during the summer.
- It is loaded with potassium, which helps lower blood pressure and maintain electrolyte balance.
- It is also easy on the stomach and prevents fatigue.
- It is a brilliant weight loss tool (100 gm of bottle gourd only has 15 calories) and has lots of fibre.

CHANGE THE WAY YOU COOK BOTTLE GOURD

Here are a few delicious lauki recipes that are also easy to cook.

Bottle Gourd Soup

Chop 1 bottle gourd, 1 carrot and 1 tomato into cubes, throw in 2 slit green chillies and pressure cook for 2 whistles with some water. Add salt, pepper and oregano to taste and blend. Top it off with 1 tbsp butter or cream. You can have it warm or even chilled as a cold soup.

Lauki Khatti Meethi

In a pressure cooker, heat 1 tbsp coconut oil and add ½ tsp mustard seeds, a pinch of methi seeds, lots of curry leaves and 2 dry red chillies. Then, add 1 chopped bottle gourd, stir-fry, add a dash of water and then pressure cook for 1 whistle. Once the pressure drops, open the cooker, add 1 tbsp desiccated coconut and ½ tsp sugar. Cook for a minute, squeeze the juice of ½ a lemon on top and eat with fresh rotis.

Peanut Bottle Gourd

Grate 1 peeled bottle gourd. Add 2 tbsp roasted powdered peanuts, ½ tsp sugar, salt to taste and mix well. Heat 1 tbsp coconut oil, add a pinch of cumin seeds, 2 sliced green chillies and the bottle gourd mixture. Cover and cook for about 10 minutes till it's done. Sprinkle some fresh coriander leaves and squeeze ½ a lemon on top just before serving.

Stuffed Bottle Gourd

Peel and half 1 small bottle gourd lengthwise. Scoop out the seeds and flesh and set them aside. Mash 1 boiled potato and season it with salt and pepper. Stuff it into the cored bottle gourd halves and set them aside. Meanwhile, grind 1 onion, 1 tomato, some garlic, a few green chillies and an inch of garlic to a paste. In a pressure cooker, heat 2 tbsp oil and cook the masala and the seeds and flesh of the bottle gourd in it. Add 1 tsp coriander powder, salt to taste, a pinch of turmeric, ½ tsp red chilli powder and a little bit of water. Then, place the stuffed bottle gourd in the masala and cook for 1 whistle. Pair with paratha.

Lauki Pilaf

Heat 1 tbsp ghee, add a pinch of cumin seeds and hing and ½ tsp garam masala. Sauté 1 grated bottle gourd and 1 tbsp desiccated coconut for a minute. Add 1 cup of rice and sauté for 4–5 minutes. Add salt to taste and 2 cups of water. Cover and cook till it's cooked through. It tastes delicious with a raita.

Lauki Cheela

Grate and mix ¼ bottle gourd to ½ cup besan and gradually stir in water to make a thick paste. Add chopped green chilli and grated ginger. Season with salt and red chilli powder. Spread over a greased hot tawa and make crisp cheelas. Serve with coriander chutney.

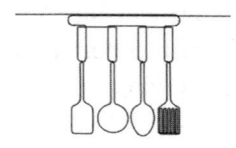

TWENTY ONE

Mushroom Delights

Where do I even begin talking about this fungi that most of us find difficult to develop a taste for? I agree that the texture and taste of mushroom may seem a little alien because both are a little different from the vegetables we are used to eating daily. But, trust me, it's time to change this attitude because ignoring this vegetable means missing out on its multiple health benefits. The Greeks and Romans ate mushrooms for strength before a battle, not without good reason.

THE BENEFITS OF MUSHROOM

Some of the immense benefits of eating mushrooms have been listed below.

- They are low in calories (250 gm of mushrooms contain just 80 calories) and contain no fat and cholesterol.
- They deliver good quality protein and have lots of the antioxidant selenium, which is usually difficult to find.
- They even prevent cancer, help reduce bad cholesterol and fortify our immunity by delivering zinc, which helps strengthen white blood cells, the soldiers of our body.
- Finally, mushrooms are a probiotic food that also strengthen our bodies from the inside by increasing our natural resistance to diseases.

CHANGE HOW YOU COOK MUSHROOMS

You can simply sauté and add mushrooms to soups, sauces, omelettes, salads or pizzas. The next time you are making a meat dish, replace half the meat with mushrooms. Their texture is similar and you'll manage to cut loads of calories, salt and saturated fat if you do this.

Here are a few delicious mushroom recipes that are also easy to cook.

Desi Chinese Chicken and Mushrooms

Add 1 tsp cornflour and 1 tsp soy sauce to 200 gm shredded boneless chicken and set it aside for 15 minutes. Meanwhile, stir-fry 200 gm halved mushrooms in sesame oil on high flame for 1 minute and set aside.

In the same oil, stir-fry the chicken on high heat for 2 minutes, add the mushrooms back along with a pinch of sugar, salt and pepper to taste and some white wine (optional). Cook for 3 minutes. Add a cup of thinly shredded vegetables, including capsicum, carrots and spring onions. Cover and cook for exactly 1 minute. Pair it with fried rice.

Coconut Mushrooms on Sourdough

Sauté 2 cloves of sliced garlic in 2 tbsp olive oil. Add 1 sliced onion and cook till it is soft and pink. Then, throw in 200 gm sliced mushrooms, sprinkle salt and herbs (oregano, thyme, paprika) to taste and cook until golden. Finish it off with 1 tbsp of coconut milk or curd, a lot of black pepper and a squeeze of lemon juice. Pile on top of toasted sourdough bread and serve.

Mushroom and Egg Toast

In a pan, heat 1 tbsp melted butter and sauté 2 cloves of garlic and 200 gm halved mushrooms in it till they're soft. Then, add 2 tbsp of tomato purée, and stir-fry till everything is coated nicely. Season with salt, pepper and oregano. Set it aside. Meanwhile, scramble 2 eggs in butter and a splash of milk; season with salt and pepper. Layer a toast with the egg, place the mushrooms on top, add some grated cheese and put it in the oven for 5 minutes on high to melt the cheese. Dig in.

Mushroom Soup, 2 Ways

- **Mushroom pasta soup**: In 1 tbsp melted butter, sauté 1 chopped onion on low flame till it is translucent. Add 200 gm sliced mushrooms and cook for 10 minutes. Pour in 1.5 cups of water or vegetable broth, salt, pepper and herbs of your choice. Cook it partially covered on sim for about 10 minutes. Let it cool before blending to the consistency of a soup. Pour back in the pot, add ½ cup of boiled pasta and a little cream. Season with a dash of chilli sauce, juliennes of ginger and spring onions and enjoy.
- **Vegetable mushroom soup**: Boil 200 gm of finely chopped mushrooms in 1.5 cups of water for about 10 minutes. Add 1 chopped green onion, ½ a capsicum and 1 tbsp cornflour mixed in water and cook for 3–4 minutes. Add salt, pepper and a squeeze of lemon juice. Garnish with some soaked, slivered almonds and chopped coriander leaves. Serve hot.

Matar Mushroom Curry

Grind 1 tomato, 1 inch ginger, 2 cloves of garlic, 1 green chilli and 6–7 cashews to a paste. Heat oil and stir-fry ½ tsp cumin seeds, 2 sliced green chillies and the ground paste in it till the paste is cooked. Season with salt, red chilli powder and garam masala to taste. Add 100 gm peas and cook for 5 minutes, then add 200 gm sliced mushrooms and cook through. Sprinkle kasuri methi on top and throw in a dash of cream. Pair with roti and serve.

Cheesy Mushrooms

In 1 tbsp heated butter, sauté lots of minced garlic and 200 gm sliced mushrooms. Add a splash of water and cook for 5 minutes. Then, add a mix of approximately 50 gm of grated cheeses—feta, cream cheese, cheddar—and cook for 5 more minutes. Garnish with 2–3 chopped spring onions, cover for 5 minutes and serve.

Crunchy Mushrooms

Get 200 gm of large mushrooms. Wash them well and remove their stems. Stuff the mushrooms with 50 gm of any soft cheese and season them with salt and pepper. (You can also stuff them with leftover keema). Dip in a batter made from maida, milk, salt and pepper and air-fry or grill. Serve with salsa.

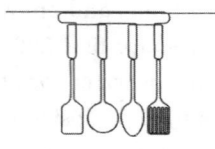

TWENTY TWO

Don't Worry, Pea Happy

Peas are a wonderful winter food, loaded with immense goodness, but are rather underrated. Most people just add them to paneer bhurjee or peas pilaf. But there's lots more you can do with this protein-packed vegetable, which can prove to be a boon for vegetarians.

THE BENEFITS OF PEAS

Peas are immensely beneficial. Some of these benefits have been listed below.

- Their high fibre content helps maintain good digestive health.
- They are a good source of iron (so they help prevent anaemia), vitamins C and E, zinc and other antioxidants that strengthen our immune system.
- They are also packed with lutein, a carotenoid pigment, which is good news for our eye health.

CHANGE HOW YOU COOK PEAS

Peas are a very versatile vegetable. Here are a few delicious pea recipes that are also easy to cook.

Peas Chaat

Boil 200 gm peas and toss them in with 1 each of a chopped onion, tomato and green chillies. Squeeze some lemon juice and sprinkle salt and chaat masala to taste. Dig in.

Peas Dip, 2 Ways

- Boil 100 gm peas, cool them and purée in a grinder. Whisk it together with 2 tbsp curd, black pepper, salt, a thinly chopped green chilli and finally, a squeeze of lemon juice.
- Grind 100 gm boiled peas with some garlic, 1 green chilli, ½ a chopped onion and some fresh coriander. Season with salt and a little sugar. Finally, drizzle some lemon juice and olive oil on it before serving.

Pair these dips with some radish or carrot slices or crackers. You can even make it a meal by pairing them with pita bread. These dips are delicious, super healthy and will add protein to your meals/snacks.

Easy Peas Pilaf

Heat 1 tbsp ghee and splutter some cumin seeds in it. Sauté 100 gm peas in it for a few minutes and set them aside. Then, heat 1 tbsp ghee in another pan, add a few peppercorns, 2 cardamom pods and 1 sliced onion. Add 1 cup of drained and washed rice, 1.5 cups of water, salt to taste and cook till almost done. Now add the sautéed peas back, cover and cook till everything is completely cooked through.

Matar Usal

Temper mustard seeds, turmeric and hing in coconut oil. Add 200 gm peas and cook on sim for 8–10 minutes with a lid on.

Keep sprinkling water on the peas from time-to-time. Meanwhile, grind 50 gm coriander leaves, 1 inch ginger, ½ tsp cumin seeds and a little water to a fine paste and add this to the peas. Season with salt and some jaggery or sugar. Pour in 1 cup of water and simmer till the peas are cooked. Garnish with 1 tbsp lemon juice and 1 tbsp grated coconut before serving.

Khoya Matar

Fry 30 gm cashews and 20 gm raisins in a bit of ghee. Set them aside. Heat 1 tbsp ghee in the pan, add ½ tsp cumin seeds and 20 gm crumbled khoya. Stir-fry till it turns light golden. Add 1 puréed tomato, a 2-inch piece of ginger and 2 green chillies and sauté for 2 minutes. Add salt, red chilli powder, turmeric and coriander powder to taste. Sauté till the ghee starts showing at the sides of the pan. Then, add 200 gm peas and fry for a few minutes. Add some water and cook it covered for another 5 minutes. Garnish with cashews and raisins. Sprinkle some garam masala on top and serve.

Peas Pongal

Make regular dal khichdi (dal and rice). Top it with fried onion rings, dry roasted cashews and boiled peas that have been stir-fried with cumin seeds and serve piping hot.

Green Soup

Boil 200 gm peas and set aside. Reserve the water they were cooking in. In 1 tbsp heated oil, sauté ½ tsp each of cumin seeds and coriander powder, 1 sliced onion and 2 garlic cloves for 5 minutes. Then, toss in the peas and cook through. Let the mixture cool before blending it to a paste. Pour into a pan and heat again with salt and pepper to taste and a splash of milk. Allow the mixture to boil. Garnish with mint leaves and cream. Savour hot with a bread of your choice.

Peas Pasta

Cook 100 gm pasta as per instructions. To it, add 100 gm boiled peas, chopped garlic, torn fresh mint leaves, toasted and sliced almonds, sliced smoked chicken (or pepperoni) and 30 gm feta or goat cheese. Add salt and pepper to taste along with a squeeze of lemon. Dig in!

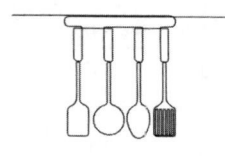

TWENTY THREE

One Potato, Two Potato

Potatoes have been around for a while now. In fact, potato remains dating back to 500 BCE were found in the ancient ruins of Peru and Chile!

We all love them. Why do you think that is? Well, to begin with, potato is mother nature's perfect comfort food.

∽

STORY TIME

Stutee Ghosh, a film critic and radio jockey, agrees that potatoes add a degree of comfort and health to every meal. 'Food is closely linked to memory and since my dad is Bengali and my mom, Punjabi, it's safe to say that I have been a foodie all my life! I have got the best of both worlds on my plate quite literally. We are what you would call Probashi Bengalis, which means Bengalis living outside of Bengal. I haven't really stayed much in Calcutta—my father and grandmother have been here in Delhi for generations, as has my mom's side of the family. But *ghar ka khana* used to be this lovely, tasty fusion of Punjabi and Bengali food, from chole to *chochhori* [a Bengali mixed vegetable]; from parathas to *luchi* and *kumro'r torkari* [pumpkin curry] and even rajma prepared with aloo, which is a very typical Bengali thing to do. My father loved aloo. So, ever since he passed away, I find it very difficult to have Bengali food because it reminds me so much of him. One food memory that I have with my father is eating simple ghar ka khana,' she shared.

She added that while Bengali cuisine is diverse, and the food is elaborate, the everyday staple that her father relished was boiled rice and aloo. 'Aloo Bhaat is a burst of flavours in your mouth. To make it, we mash boiled rice and aloo together with salt and butter or ghee. Then, we press this mixture into small, round balls that we call *gorosh* in Bangla. You know this can be a meal in itself but it's also just the first course before we move on to dal, fish and other stuff. When I was little, my dad's official car used to come to pick him up. Being an enthucutlet, I would hop out of the house and see if the driver had come. As a reward, I'd get a gorosh of aloo bhaat. That bite of mashed rice and potatoes and *namak* and *makkhan*—it was divine. Years later, even when I'd be on all sorts of low carbohydrate and no carbohydrate diets, the aloo bhaat my dad fed me remained sacred,' she reminisced.

THE BENEFITS OF POTATOES

Potatoes provide immense benefits. I've listed some of them below.

- One medium potato, weighing around 150 gm has just 116 calories and is a terrific way to stock up on fibre (around 3 gm fibre in 150 gm potato), which keeps you full for long. Unless it is loaded with fats, like butter, sour cream, melted cheese and bacon bits, it is a low-calorie food. In fact, much of the potato's bad

reputation actually comes from its accompaniments or the way it is cooked, which make it a high-calorie and fatty food.
- Potatoes deliver some protein—250 gm potatoes contain 3 gm protein.
- They are high in magnesium and potassium—a powerful pair that helps lower blood pressure.
- They contain phosphorous, which is crucial for bone health.
- The antioxidant count or the Oxygen Radical Absorbance Capacity (ORAC value), which quantifies the total antioxidant capacity of a food, of potatoes is fairly high.
- They can be served any time of the day—breakfast, lunch, dinner and as snacks.
- They can be cooked any way you want—stand alone, with any vegetables or meat, in healthy low-calorie recipes or even sinfully, like the French fries we all love.
- They can be oven-baked, roasted, boiled, steamed or even fried. They're a treat that can complete our meal.

CHANGE HOW YOU COOK POTATOES

With potatoes, the food is not really the devil! How you cook potatoes—whether you choose a healthy low-calorie recipe or a sinfully fried one—is what matters. When cooked right, potatoes can be really good for you.

Here are a few delicious potato recipes from across the country to spice up your menus.

Odia Sada Aloor Chorchori

Heat 1 tbsp mustard oil in a pan, add a pinch of kalonji and 2–3 torn dried red chillies. Add 2 sliced potatoes and stir on high heat for a minute or two. Add salt and black pepper to taste and just enough water to cover the potatoes. Cover and cook till the potatoes are tender. Keep adding water as needed until the potatoes are cooked. Serve hot.

These potatoes in a mild, thin gravy are a perfect comfort food and pair well with everything, from rice to dosas to rotis.

Amritsari Aloo ki Launji

Heat 1 tbsp oil and add a pinch each of hing, methi and fennel seeds pounded coarsely in a mortar and pestle. Add 2 boiled, coarsely mashed boiled potatoes followed by ½ tsp each of turmeric, red chilli and coriander powders. Season with 1 tsp tamarind paste, 1 tsp sugar and salt to taste. Finally, pour in some water. Cover and cook on low heat for a few minutes before serving.

Maharashtrian Batata Bhaji

Heat 1 tbsp oil in a pan, add ½ tsp mustard seeds, ½ tsp cumin seeds, a pinch of hing and a few curry leaves; let them crackle for a few seconds. Add 1 sliced onion, 2–3 green chillies, ½ an inch of ginger and 3 cloves of garlic, and sauté until the onion turns slightly brown. Stir-fry 5–6 cashew nuts or peanuts or both and ½ tsp turmeric powder for a few seconds. Add 2 boiled and chopped potatoes, salt and sugar to taste, and cook for 3–4 minutes. Garnish with some coriander leaves and lemon juice before serving.

This popular Maharashtrian aloo dish is lightly spiced and pairs perfectly with *pav* and puris.

Assamese Aloo Pitika

Mash 2 boiled potatoes and mix (preferably by hand) 1 sliced onion and 1 tsp mustard oil with it. Season with salt and chopped green chillies to taste. Garnish with coriander leaves.

Kerala Spicy Potato Curry

Heat 1 tbsp coconut oil in a pan. Add 1 finely chopped onion, 2 sliced green chillies, salt to taste and fry till the onion is slightly translucent. Add 2 cubed potatoes and sauté for 2 minutes. Add ½ tsp each of red chilli, coriander and turmeric powders along with some water. Lower the flame, cover and cook till the potatoes soften and the water reduces. Then, add 100 ml coconut milk and 1 tsp fennel powder and cook till the curry thickens.

This rich dish is very comforting and pairs well with *idiyappam*, appam or naan.

Parsi Papeta Par Eeda

Boil 2 potatoes until they are cooked through but still firm and dice them. Sauté them lightly with 1 tsp each of garlic and ginger paste and 2 chopped green chillies. Transfer the mixture to a shallow, greased, ovenproof dish and break 2 eggs over them. Cook at 177 °C until the eggs are set.

Alternatively, you can do this in a covered frying pan, putting the lid on and lowering the heat as soon as the eggs have been added. Cook until the eggs are just set.

Potato Water

Wash and dice a large potato. Steep it overnight in 1 cup of water along with a pinch of sea salt. Strain and drink the water every morning on an empty stomach. This is great for cleansing the gastrointestinal system.

Potato Chaat, 2 Ways

- Mix 2 boiled and diced potatoes with 2 tbsp crushed *chivda* (rice flakes) or papad, 1 tbsp tamarind sauce, 1 tbsp curd, a handful of sprouts (or boiled chana) and a

few slices of cucumber. Add a few strips of paneer or feta (optional). Chill for 30 minutes and dig in!
- Make a mixed fruit and potato chaat with boiled sweet or regular potato, guava, cucumber and pomegranate seeds (to make about a quarter plate). Add a large handful of boiled chana, some curd for protein and tamarind paste for a bit of tang. Finally, sprinkle with some sunflower seeds and serve.

Warm Spicy Potato Salad

Mix 2 boiled and cooked potatoes, 1 sliced onion, 1 chopped green chilli, 1 chopped cucumber with 1 tbsp mustard oil and salt to taste and set it aside. Heat 1 tsp oil and splutter 1 tsp black sesame seeds in it. Turn off the heat and pour over the salad. Toss gently and serve.

Creamy Potato Egg Mix

Mix 1 boiled and diced potato, 1 boiled and diced egg, ½ a diced onion and salt and pepper to taste. Whisk together 1 tbsp mayonnaise, 1 tsp vinegar, ½ tsp mustard, 1 tsp of any spicy sauce and salt and pepper to taste. Mix, chill and eat.

Potato Stew

To a pressure cooker, add two chopped potatoes, ½ a sliced onion, 3 crushed garlic cloves, a small chunk of sliced ginger, 1 sliced tomato, 1 clove, a tiny piece of cinnamon, ½ an inch of bay leaf, 1 crushed cardamom and salt and pepper to taste. Add 2 cups of water. Cook on medium flame for 1 whistle. Pour a tadka made in 1 tsp mustard oil with curry leaves and sesame seeds on top and serve.

Peri Peri Potatoes

To make the peri peri sauce, grind 2 dry red chillies, 1 tsp olive oil, 1 tsp vinegar, a few stalks of coriander, ½ a red capsicum and salt. Cut 2 boiled potatoes into thick slices. Smear a pan with butter and cook the potato slices coated in the peri peri sauce on both sides till they're done. Have a salad with greens or a mixed vegetable stir-fry as a side.

Curd and Sesame Potato Gratin

Combine 1 cup of curd, ½ cup of tahini and 2 chopped green chillies in a blender to make a paste that has the consistency of a dosa batter. Add a little milk if it is too thick. Set it aside. Slice 2 boiled potatoes into ½ inch thick rounds, arrange in a single layer on a greased baking tray. Pour the blended curd mixture over the potato layer, spreading it evenly with a spatula. Bake in a preheated oven at 160 °C for about 15 minutes until the moisture has dried out before serving hot.

Potato Energy Balls

Soak ¼ cup of *sabudana* (sago pearls) for about 2 hours in just enough water to cover it. Drain the water and keep it in the refrigerator overnight. Add 300 gm boiled mashed potato, along with 1 slice of bread to the sabudana the next morning. Then, mix in ¼ cup each of grated carrot, boiled peas, chopped spinach and onions, 1 tsp raisins, 2 tsp dried melon seeds and 1 tsp amchoor powder. Shape the mixture into round balls. Heat oil in a non-stick pan and shallow-fry or air-fry the balls till they are golden brown.

Honey Baby Potatoes

Heat 2 tbsp oil and fry 250 gm baby potatoes until they are brown. Set them aside. Heat 1 tbsp oil separately in a non-stick pan and sauté ½ tsp ginger garlic paste in it till it turns brown. Add 1 tsp sesame seeds (either white or black), ¼ tsp each of soy, red chilli and tomato sauces, the fried potatoes and salt and pepper to taste. Cook for 1 minute. Drizzle 2 tbsp honey and sprinkle 1 tbsp roasted peanut powder to finish it off. Mix well and serve.

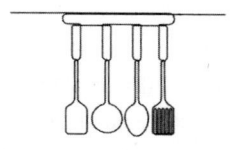

TWENTY FOUR

Pumpkin Is Not Just for Halloween

The ubiquitous pumpkin is now more associated with Halloween, but it has been a huge part of the Indian cuisine since forever. In fact, it is usually cooked as part of the food that is served after a puja in Hindu homes. Still, there aren't many people who eat pumpkin regularly and fewer still who actually relish it.

STORY TIME

Kishi Arora, a TED fellow, chefpreneur and alumni of the Culinary Institute of America, shared that she did not like many vegetables as a child. In fact, she disliked pumpkin, eggplant and bhindi the most. But her move to the USA changed her. She missed her mom's home-made food, and she started craving all the 'bland' vegetables she had hated as a child. 'One of the dishes that I cooked first while I was in the USA was butternut squash but in an Indian style. Now, I love pumpkins so much that I have grown my own in my terrace garden,' she shared.

Celebrity chef **Manish Mehrotra** also shared a delightful childhood memory about pumpkin. 'I come from a vegetarian household, so pumpkin was made very often. I would never eat it as a child, but I have a very nice memory attached to this vegetable. When I was growing up, there were no fancy stores selling pumpkin seeds. So, I would collect pumpkin seeds, wash and dry them with my grandmother on the terrace. Then, I would peel them and she would roast them with a little salt. They were absolutely delicious, and till today, I remember them every time I see a pumpkin,' he remembered.

THE BENEFITS OF PUMPKIN

You should have fun with the pumpkin on your plate. I believe that this vegetable is perfect for our health. I have listed some of its many benefits below.

- It has an extremely low-calorie count (just 26 calories per 100 gm).
- It is loaded with fibre, which keeps your gut happy.
- It contains a lot of vitamin A, which keeps our eyes strong and also has anti-cancer properties.
- It has potassium, which is an important electrolyte that keeps our muscles functioning at their best.
- It also provides vitamin C, which helps ward off colds.

STORY TIME

Subha J. Rao, a Mangalore-based journalist and founder of a range of home-roasted, home-ground artisanal spice mixes,

Made In Mangalore By Subha (madeinmangalore.in), said, 'You can do a lot with pumpkin. During my years working in Coimbatore, my fellow journalist, colleague and friend Pankaja Srinivasan and I would delight in the fresh produce that would arrive in the markets from farms at 5 in the evening. We would stand and watch as the shopkeeper near our office would open the gunny bags from which peeked shiny purple brinjals or bright orange carrots. The contents of those gunny bags would determine the next day's lunch. When it was red pumpkins and ash gourds (*safed petha*), it was *olan* time. It's a simple preparation. Just cut the pumpkin and the ash gourd into thin slivers and cook on a low flame with one slit green chilli and some salt. Once they are firm but cooked, pour in a cupful of coconut milk (freshly extracted or from a pack, both work). Temper with coconut oil and mustard seeds. It's soothing, flavourful and packed with fibre.'

CHANGE HOW YOU COOK PUMPKIN

There are multiple other ways to cook pumpkin. You can add puréed pumpkin to smoothies and soups, mix it into oats, stir it into plain curd and top it with cinnamon or even whisk it into cheesy pasta sauces. Try out some new things with this extremely versatile vegetable. Here are a few delicious pumpkin recipes that are also easy to cook.

Lentil and Pumpkin Soup

Boil 1 cup *masoor dal* (red lentil) with a little salt till it gets soft. Marinate 250 gm cubed pumpkin in coconut oil and salt and roast in a preheated oven for 5 minutes at 200 °C.

Heat a bit of coconut oil and temper curry leaves in it. Add ½ a chopped onion, a few crushed garlic cloves, ½ an inch of ginger, 2 green chillies, ½ tsp each of coriander, cumin and curry powder to it. Sauté until the masalas are cooked. Stir the boiled dal and cooked pumpkin into the mixture and purée it in a blender. Gradually pour in water or vegetable stock until the mixture reaches the desired consistency of a soup. Season with salt and sip warm.

Pumpkin Salad, 2 Ways

- **Cold pumpkin salad**: Steam 200 gm cubed pumpkin and mix it with 1 apple and some lettuce. Dress the salad with 1 tbsp olive oil, ginger juliennes, 1 tbsp pumpkin seeds and some lemon juice. Serve cold.
- **Warm pumpkin salad**: To 200 gm boiled and cubed pumpkin, add 2 tbsp grated fresh coconut, 2 tbsp curd, some finely chopped coriander leaves, ground black pepper and salt to taste. Make a tadka in 1 tbsp oil with a pinch each of cumin seeds, mustard seeds and hing, 1 chopped green chilli and a few curry leaves. Mix it up with the pumpkin. Garnish with roasted and crushed peanuts and serve.

Quick Pumpkin Stir-Fry

Mix 200 gm each of steamed broccoli, roasted pumpkin and 1 sliced and caramelized onion. Add spices or herbs that you prefer, and season with salt and pepper before serving.

Coconut Pumpkin Sabzi

Boil 500 gm pumpkin cubes in some water. When the pumpkin is almost done, drain and set it aside. In a pan, heat some oil, splutter a pinch each of mustard and cumin seeds and sauté

1 sliced onion in it till it is golden brown. Add a chopped tomato and sauté it for a few minutes. Blend 1 tsp each of coriander seeds, turmeric and red chilli powder, garlic paste, ginger paste, fresh or dried coconut, and ¼ tsp garam masala powder with a splash of water into a thick paste. Pour it into the cooked masala and let the mixture cook for a couple of minutes. Toss the boiled pumpkin pieces in along with salt to taste and cook for another 5 minutes. Adjust the water according to your preferred consistency. Garnish with coriander leaves and pair with roti.

Simplest Pumpkin Sabzi

Cut 500 gm pumpkin into medium-sized cubes. Heat a little oil, splutter sumin and methi seeds and red chillies. Sauté the cubed pumpkin in it for a bit. Add ½ a tsp each of cumin powder, coriander powder, amchoor powder, red chilli powder, and salt to taste. Stir, cover and cook till the pumpkin pieces are tender. Splash water at intervals if need be.

Pumpkin Risotto

Heat oil in a pan and add 1 chopped onion and a few garlic cloves. Add 1 cup of risotto rice and sauté it for a minute. Add 1.5 cup hot vegetable stock or water to the rice and cook till it is al dente. Add 25 gm mascarpone (or any other) cheese and 25 gm butter to the risotto and cook while stirring it. Add 200 gm chopped and roasted pumpkin to the risotto; season with salt and pepper. Garnish with 1 tbsp chopped parsley, 1 tbsp grated Parmesan cheese and 1 tbsp chopped and toasted walnuts and serve.

Pumpkin Bake with Feta

Toss 300 gm cubed pumpkin and quartered onion with 1 tbsp oil, 1 tsp honey, 1 tsp vinegar, red pepper flakes, salt and pepper to taste. Bake in a preheated oven at 200 °C for 20 to 25 minutes or until caramelized and tender. Garnish with 50 gm feta cheese and dig in.

One Pot Chicken and Pumpkin Rice

In a pot, heat oil and sauté 1 sliced onion and a few garlic cloves for a minute. Add 100 gm cubed chicken and cook till the pieces have browned. Add 1.5 cup water, 1 cup rice, 200 gm cubed pumpkin, salt and pepper. Bring to a boil, then reduce the heat to low, cover the pot and simmer until the water is absorbed and the rice is cooked. Stir in 100 gm chopped spinach, cover and cook until it wilts. Sprinkle some Parmesan on top and serve.

∞

CHEF MANISH MEHROTRA'S PUMPKIN AND COCONUT SHORBA

Ingredients: 500 gm peeled and chopped red pumpkin, 100 ml coconut milk, 30 gm sliced onion, 10 gm chopped fresh ginger, 10 gm chopped garlic, 5 gm green chilli, 5 gm fennel seeds, 1 bay leaf, salt to taste

Method: In a heavy bottom pan, place all the ingredients, except coconut milk and add water to cover the pumpkin. Bring to a boil and simmer till the pumpkin is cooked. Remove the bay leaf and blend. Boil the pumpkin purée and add coconut milk to it. Adjust the seasoning and consistency. Strain it through a fine sieve. Serve hot.

TWENTY FIVE

Super Spinach

Whether you like spinach or not, this is a leafy green that you must eat at least 2–3 times a week when it is in season because it is a superfood loaded with goodness.

STORY TIME

Neeraj Chopra, javelin player and Olympic champion, said he likes a lot of different kinds of food, especially all kinds of vegetarian dishes. That said, he was very clear about his childhood favourites. 'There is no contest there at all. When I was small, I would often wake up at night, hungry. At home, we had a lot of cattle, so my grandmother or mother would boil milk, let it cool down, sweeten it and store it. They would feed me that milk at night. This is something I remember very fondly. Another very healthy food I remember from my growing up years in my village is freshly grown spinach. Spinach, prepared especially during the winters, is very healthy and even today, I remember its fresh, delicious taste. When I visit my village now, I make sure I have lots of dishes made with palak for sure. These foods are really close to my heart,' he shared.

THE BENEFITS OF SPINACH

Spinach has many health benefits. Some of them have been listed below.

- It contains thylakoids (green leaf membranes) that help control cravings. So, it is a brilliant weight loss food.
- It has good amounts of vitamin K, calcium and magnesium—all are bone health supportive nutrients. So, this green wonder can keep our bones in good shape even as we age.
- It is a hydrating food because of its exceptionally high water content.

Cooking tip 1: Spinach is best had after it has been boiled in an uncovered pot for 1 minute, as this helps release the oxalic acid from it and ensures better availability of nutrients. This process also makes spinach taste sweeter.

Cooking tip 2: Always pair spinach with a vitamin C-rich food, like kiwi, orange, amla, tamarind and kokum, as it helps better absorb the iron from spinach.

CHANGE HOW YOU COOK SPINACH

Spinach is extremely versatile and easy to cook. Here are a few delicious spinach recipes.

Cold Spinach Salad

Blanch 200 gm spinach in hot water. Squeeze it dry. Make a dressing with 1 tbsp white wine vinegar, 1 tbsp olive oil and a pinch of mustard. Add ¼ each of a sliced cucumber and carrot, along with a few orange or kiwi slices. Season with salt and pepper to taste. Chill and serve.

Curry Spinach

Wash and finely chop 250 gm spinach and cook in pressure cooker with some water. Heat 1 tbsp oil, add a pinch of mustard and methi seeds, hing, a few curry leaves, and 2–3 dry red chillies. Add 1 chopped onion and sauté for a few minutes. Add strained tamarind or kokum water (about ½ an inch of tamarind soaked in ¼ cup water) and spinach. Season with salt to taste and cook for a few minutes. Toss in a pinch of jaggery and ½ tsp sambar powder and cook for a few minutes. Pair with rice.

Dal Palak

Pressure cook ½ cup of soaked chana dal till it's soft. Blend 100 gm boiled spinach and set aside. In 1 tbsp coconut oil, add 1 bay leaf, ½ tsp cumin seeds, a few roasted peanuts, 2 green chillies, 1 tsp ginger garlic paste, ½ a chopped onion and tomato each and salt and garam masala to taste. Then, stir in the cooked dal. Next, pour in the blended spinach, a little water and bring to a boil. Sprinkle amchoor on top and serve.

Spinach Smoothie

Blend 100 gm baby spinach, 1 segmented and deseeded orange, a pinch of cinnamon and 200 ml coconut water or coconut milk. Sweeten with some honey and serve.

Crunchy Spinach Salad

Tear 100 gm mixed lettuce and 100 gm raw baby spinach into bite-sized pieces. Add a few halved walnuts, segments of a citrus fruit of choice (orange, kiwi, etc.) and mix. To make the dressing, whisk 1 tbsp white wine vinegar, 1 tbsp olive (or sesame) oil, some crushed garlic, pepper, salt and mustard sauce to taste together. Pour the dressing over the salad, toss and serve.

Palak Thepla

In a bowl, mix 100 gm raw, thinly shredded spinach, 100 gm whole wheat flour, some chopped green chillies, a few crushed garlic cloves, ½ tsp each of turmeric, coriander, cumin and red chilli powders and salt to taste. Knead into a stiff dough using some water (or curd). Roll it into thin *theplas*. Cook both sides on a non-stick tawa. Smear a little ghee on it and serve.

Pasta with Chickpeas and Baby Spinach

Boil 100 gm pasta and set it aside. Heat 1 tbsp olive oil (or sesame oil), add 2 sliced onions, lots of chopped garlic and salt to taste. Cook for 3–4 minutes and set aside. In the same pan, add 100 gm baby spinach, ½ cup boiled chickpeas, 1 chopped tomato and pour in some water. Simmer for 2–3 minutes or till the spinach is cooked and the tomatoes are soft. Add the boiled pasta, salt, black pepper and red chilli flakes to taste; toss to coat the pasta with the vegetables and serve.

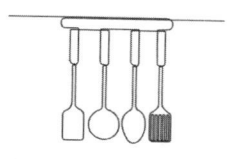

TWENTY SIX

Awesome Zucchini

We all must learn to love zucchini because this underrated vegetable is really good for us. Grown in Italy some 300 years ago for the first time, the word 'zucchini' comes from 'zucca', the Italian word for squash. Did you know that in Ohio, people celebrate a zucchini festival every year in August? Now, of course, this summer crop, which likes direct sunlight and warmth, is grown in India extensively as well.

THE BENEFITS OF ZUCCHINI

The benefits of eating zucchini are manifold. Some of them have been listed below.

- Zucchini is 95 per cent water and it is fat- and cholesterol-free. Thus, it is extremely low-calorie, making it a dieter's friend. A medium-sized zucchini (approximately 200 gm) has just 30 calories as compared to, let's say, potato, which has 160 calories per 200 gm.
- It is loaded with electrolyte potassium, which helps counter the ill-effects of too much sodium in our diet and keeps blood pressure in control.
- It is heart-friendly. The fibre, vitamin C and A content in zucchini work in tandem to keep heart disease at bay.
- Zucchini rind contains an essential vitamin called

beta-carotene. So, don't peel it before cooking. Just wash it thoroughly and dig in!

CHANGE HOW YOU COOK ZUCCHINI

Now you know how healthy zucchini is, but you may not be sure how to cook it because it is a slightly unfamiliar vegetable. Zucchini is similar to bottle gourd. So, you can experiment and make your bottle gourd recipes with zucchini and see which ones work for you. Here are a few delicious zucchini recipes that are also easy to cook.

Zucchini Salad

Sprinkle salt on 500 gm sliced zucchini and let it sit for at least 10 minutes—this will draw out some liquid. Pat dry with paper towels to prevent it from turning completely mushy when you cook it. In some heated olive or coconut oil, sauté lots of garlic cloves, the zucchini and a pinch of salt until the zucchini has softened. Remove this mixture in a bowl, mix in 200 gm asparagus sautéed separately in oil or butter, 2 chopped raw spring onions, some sticks of steamed carrots and a handful of sweet corn kernels. Sprinkle pepper, some dried oregano and 50 gm cheese (ricotta works well with this) and dig in.

Crisp Zucchini Pancakes

Soak 1 cup of dal overnight (I make it with masoor dal). In the morning, drain the water, blend the dal to a paste in a mixer. Meanwhile, let 500 gm chopped zucchini sit for at least 10 minutes with salt to draw out some of its liquid. Mix in 1 sliced onion, lots of coriander leaves, 1 mashed potato, a pinch of garam masala and salt and red chillies to taste. Then, heat some ghee in a pan, spread the batter, press it down to make thin, small pancakes, cook on low heat, flipping till they are golden brown on both sides. If you don't want to fry them, you can even add some ghee to the mix, shape the batter in the form of small patties and bake them for about 15 minutes, flipping after 8 minutes. Serve with a mint–coriander chutney.

Grilled Zucchini

Toss 500 gm halved zucchini with salt and let it sit for at least 10 minutes to draw out some of its liquid. Pat dry with paper towels. Mix 1 tbsp vinegar, 1 tbsp chilli sauce, herbs of your choice and 1 tbsp oil. Spread the mix on the zucchini, grill on both sides in a preheated oven (200 °C) for about 3 minutes. Squeeze some lemon juice on top and dig in.

Zucchini Salsa

Mix 250 gm finely chopped zucchini, ½ an onion, ½ a tomato and ½ a red pepper. Add 1 tbsp lemon juice, 1 tbsp vinegar, 1 tbsp brown sugar or jaggery, lots of pounded garlic, salt, pepper and roasted cumin powder to taste. Mix it well and refrigerate overnight. Next day, eat with your toast or tortillas or even spread on your roti (with sliced cucumbers) to make a roti roll.

Quick Zucchini Pasta

Toss 500 gm sliced zucchini with salt and let it sit for at least 10 minutes. Heat some olive or coconut oil, sauté lots of garlic cloves, add the zucchini, a pinch of salt and cook until softened. Then, toss in 1 cup of boiled pasta with the seared zucchini (take both in 1:1 ratio). Sprinkle a handful of freshly grated cheese (gouda or Parmesan) along with some raisins and roasted seeds on top and dig in.

Zucchini Omelette

Sprinkle salt on 100 gm sliced zucchini and let it sit for at least 10 minutes to draw out some liquid. Then, pat it dry with paper towels. This prevents the zucchini from turning too mushy when you cook it. In heated olive or coconut oil, sauté lots of garlic cloves, the zucchini and a pinch of salt until the zucchini has softened. Meanwhile, beat 2 eggs with a pinch of salt, pepper and a handful of freshly grated cheese. When the zucchini is almost cooked, pour the egg batter over it, cover and cook. Flip and cook for a few more minutes till the omelette is cooked on both sides and serve.

Zucchini Bake

Mix 500 gm grated zucchini, 1 finely chopped bell pepper, 1 thinly sliced onion, 100 gm grated cheese (Parmesan or cheddar), 100 gm sliced mushrooms, 2 whisked eggs, 25 gm butter, 1 tbsp of milk or cream, a sprinkle of maida and salt and pepper to taste. Let this mixture sit for 30 minutes before baking it in a preheated oven (200 °C) for about 20 minutes.

Zucchini in Coconut Milk

Heat 1 tbsp coconut oil and add a pinch each of mustard and methi seeds, a few curry leaves and 1 chopped onion to it. Cook till the onion is translucent. Add 500 gm chopped raw zucchini (you can add other vegetables too) and cook till they are soft. Add 3 tbsp coconut milk, bring to a boil and season with salt and pepper. Switch off the heat, leave covered for 5 minutes. Pair with roti or appam.

Zucchini and Potato Pancake

Grate 100 gm potato and 100 gm zucchini. Season with salt and black pepper to taste and a pinch of grated nutmeg. Heat a pan, add olive oil, pour the mix into it and shallow-fry on both sides till it becomes crisp. Make 2 pancakes this way and serve.

Stuffed Zucchini and Potato Bake

Steam 2 medium-sized whole zucchinis for 5–7 minutes just to soften them up a bit. Cool and half the zucchini, lengthwise. Scoop out the seeds and set them aside. To 100 gm cooked and minced chicken, add a torn bread that has been soaked in milk, an egg, some grated cheese, salt, pepper and olive oil. Stir well to combine all of the ingredients and fill the mix into the scooped out zucchini. Drizzle a little extra virgin olive oil on a baking tray, place the stuffed zucchinis, add (boiled) potato wedges, drizzle oil, salt and herbs. Sprinkle some cheese on top and bake for 20 minutes.

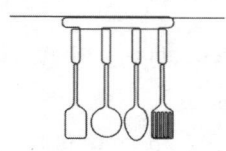

TWENTY SEVEN

The French Bean Wonder

Most of us don't eat enough fibre, and if you are a vegetarian, then chances are that protein is short-changed in your diet as well. A simple solution for this dilemma is to eat French beans more often, especially during winter, when they are in season, amazingly fresh and extremely pocket-friendly too.

THE BENEFITS OF FRENCH BEANS

Some of the immense benefits of eating French beans have been listed below.

- Besides giving us enough fibre to protect us against heart disease, high cholesterol, high blood pressure and digestive issues, beans also contain a lot of protein (5 gm per 250 gm).
- They help lower low-density lipoprotein (LDL), which is 'bad' cholesterol. So, they are good for our heart too.
- They are rich in RS and are brilliant for our gut health.
- They also help keep our sugar levels and weight in check.
- Finally, French beans contain iron, magnesium, potassium, zinc and folate.

CHANGE HOW YOU COOK FRENCH BEANS

These wonder beans are versatile; you can add them to soups, fried rice, noodles, sambar, pav bhaji. Alternatively, try these delicious recipes to make them part of your menus more regularly.

Coconut Beans

Heat 2 tbsp coconut oil in a pan and temper some mustard seeds in it. Add 1 sliced onion and stir-fry till it's golden. Sauté 250 gm sliced French beans for 5–7 minutes. Add 30 gm raw peanuts, 30 gm grated coconut, salt to taste and a splash of water, if required. Cover and cook for 15 minutes. Add 1 sliced tomato and cook without covering for 5 more minutes.

Garlicky Beans

In 2 tbsp sesame or olive oil, stir-fry some cumin seeds and lots of garlic for 1 minute. Toss in 250 gm chopped French beans, salt and chilli powder to taste. Cover the pan and let the beans cook until they are tender, for about 10–12 minutes, stirring occasionally. Add a splash of water until the beans have cooked through. It makes for a perfect evening snack and pairs well with rice too.

Simple Steamed Beans

Chop and steam 250 gm French beans till they are soft enough to eat but still crunchy. Toss them in 1 tbsp of gunpowder, 1 tsp of flaxseed powder and salt and red chilli flakes to taste. Add 30 gm crushed peanuts, 1 tbsp toasted sesame seeds and a squeeze of lemon juice. Make it a meal with roti and curd, or just snack on it with a cracker or two.

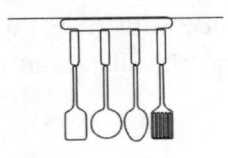

TWENTY EIGHT

Brilliant Broccoli

Did you know that broccoli is essentially an edible flower, not strictly a vegetable? Broccoli can be clearly traced back to Italy. Apicius, the ancient Roman cookbook author, prepared it way back in the late fourth century CE by boiling it, brushing it with a mixture of cumin and coriander seeds and then frying it with a chopped onion in a few drops of oil and wine. It sounds delicious, doesn't it? Unfortunately, not many people like to eat this vegetable somehow. I don't blame them. Its taste takes some getting used to. But if there is one food that we must make a conscious effort to include in our meals, it is broccoli. You can stay lean and healthy with this underrated food.

THE BENEFITS OF BROCCOLI

Eating broccoli is immensely healthy. Some of its benefits have been listed below.

- It provides a nutritional punch while being a low-calorie food. 1 cup of broccoli (about 100 gm) has just 34 calories.
- It is packed with calcium, which is crucial for bone building, and beta-carotene, which is good for our eyes.
- It is also loaded with fibre. Approximately 250 gm contains 100 calories along with whooping 8–10 gm of fibre.

- A cup of broccoli has more vitamin C than even an orange—enough to take care of your daily requirement for this nutrient. Vitamin C is a great immunity booster and helps the body absorb the iron in broccoli.
- It is a disease fighter—vitamin C protects the body from ravaging free radicals and stops the hardening of arteries. It is, therefore, a great friend of your heart, and a strong weapon against cancer.
- It is a great detoxifier, as it is loaded with phytochemicals. Broccoli boosts enzymes that detoxify the body and helps prevent cancer, diabetes, heart disease, osteoporosis and high blood pressure.

CHANGE HOW YOU COOK BROCCOLI

Broccoli can be put to various uses—make it the centrepiece of your salad, stir-fry it, grill or steam it and enjoy it with a dip or blend it with garlic, extra virgin olive oil and seasonings to make an interesting sauce. Here are a few delicious broccoli recipes that are also easy to cook.

Quick Broccoli Snack

Grate 1.5 cups of broccoli, ½ cup of cheddar cheese (or paneer) and 2 crumbled bread slices. Add a tbsp of milk, mix a little salt and pepper and form into balls. Grill or pan-fry.

Broccoli Mix

Steam 250 gm broccoli, 100 gm cherry tomatoes, 100 gm French beans and 100 gm baby corn. Toss in 1 tbsp of olive oil, a few cloves of garlic, season with salt, pepper and rosemary to taste. Drizzle lemon juice or vinegar and sprinkle some shredded Parmesan on top before serving.

Cheesy Broccoli

Stir-fry broccoli in a little bit of olive oil on high heat for a few minutes. Add finely chopped garlic, cook for a few minutes. Add chilli flakes, fresh basil leaves and salt, cover and cook till the broccoli is done. Sprinkle some cheese on top. Cover for about a minute till the cheese melts and serve.

Broccoli Soup

Heat 1 tbsp butter, add a few chopped garlic pods, 1 chopped onion and 250 gm broccoli and sauté for 2–3 minutes. Pour in 2 cups of water, a few soaked almonds, salt to taste, 1 bay leaf, cover and boil for 10 minutes on sim. Cool, remove the bay leaf and grind. Transfer to a bowl, add a little melted butter on top, season with salt, pepper and cinnamon powder and serve.

Grilled Broccoli

Boil water in a pan with salt. Blanch 200 gm broccoli in it. Strain and shock the broccoli in iced water to prevent discolouration. To prepare the marinade, in a pan, whisk together 50 gm cheese with 100 gm hung curd till it is creamy. Add 1 tbsp *kasundi* (mustard paste) and 1 tsp turmeric powder. Marinate the broccoli in this paste for 15 minutes. Skewer the broccoli and grill it in a *tandoor* (or a griller) for 15 minutes. Garnish with julienned ginger and chopped coriander before serving.

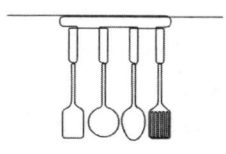

Part 5

The Fruits Shelf

We eat badly. There is no doubt about that. We eat too many empty calories in the form of processed food, and we do not have nearly as many fruits as we should. As a weight management and wellness practitioner, I, more often than not, find at least 8 out of 10 people either not eating any fruits at all or eating a token fruit a day. Most people tend to stick to the limited number of fruits they like or can tolerate.

There are many compelling reasons to begin eating more fruits. Some of their benefits have been listed below:

- Fruits have a high fibre content, which helps reduce constipation.
- Their sweet taste satisfies cravings in a healthy manner.
- Some fruits may have anti-cancer properties.
- They can help you lose weight and, therefore, are heart-healthy
- Finally, fruits have detoxing qualities because they are loaded with free radicals and antioxidants.

The connection between intelligence, memory, cognition and a nutrient-rich diet, which includes fruits, has almost been established now. Those who eat fruits have bigger and more efficient brains than those who don't. This makes sense because eating fruits provides easily digestable calories that energize the brain. Isn't that a huge incentive to eat fruits?

We need to make all fruits exciting. Get creative, make your own rituals with different fruits and make them an intrinsic part of your diet!

TWENTY NINE

Banana Treats

My suggestion to everyone who comes to me for nutrition advice is to eat a banana every day. It surprises everyone, but it always works. Athletes vouch for it for a reason.

∽

STORY TIME

Charu Sharma, an Indian commentator, compere, quizmaster and director of the famous Pro Kabaddi League, has a fun banana story to share. When he was studying at St Stephen's College in Delhi in the mid-seventies, his college did not have a pool but had a big swim team. Charu, who was the national springboard diving champion, would go to a swimming pool with the rest of the team members. 'I have a lot of lovely memories there. We used to go to the pool early in the morning—leave at 5.20 a.m., reach at 6 a.m. and train for some time every day. The college budget allowed us to go back to college in taxies. On the way back, our team captain would buy 12 bananas for me from the budget and I would finish it by the time we reached college. Then, I would eat a big breakfast too before going to college. I remember telling my eleven- and eight-year-old sons this story and they thought it was nonsense, and I was making it all up. Who can have 12 bananas and then a breakfast too? They would laugh every time. Then, one day, a college friend visited our home and mentioned this story and their jaws dropped. After that they looked at me with different eyes,' Charu added.

THE BENEFITS OF BANANAS

Are you someone who craves sweets a bit too much? Do you struggle with the nagging thought that you shouldn't actually have sweets, as they might make you put on weight and lead to your blood sugar going haywire? Bananas are the perfect solution for you!

There are lots of benefits that bananas deliver in all their forms—unripe, just ripe enough or overripe. Have it in all forms to gain the maximum benefits out of this fabulous fruit. Some of their benefits have been listed below.

- Bananas have the right kinds of carbohydrates that instantly energize the body.
- They contain 3 natural sugars—sucrose, fructose and glucose—along with an extra-large dose of fibre. So, they give us an instant boost along with sustained and substantial energy.
- They also have high iron content, which stimulates haemoglobin production and helps keep fatigue away.
- Bananas are very rich in potassium. They also deliver loads of the immunity-boosting vitamins C and A.
- Overripe bananas are easier to digest and can help prevent heartburn by keeping acidity in check. In fact, they work as a natural and nutritious antacid.

- When a banana becomes too ripe, its peel turns darker. The dark spots on the peel create tumour necrosis factor (TNF), a substance that can kill cancerous and abnormal cells.
- Raw bananas promote digestion, prevent constipation and function as a natural mood enhancer.
- Raw bananas are also rich in RS, the third, lesser-known type of fibre that our food provides. Thus, they are a superfood for our digestive system.

CHANGE HOW YOU COOK WITH BANANAS

If you are wondering how you will manage to eat a banana every day without getting bored, here are a few super easy, healthy desserts made with banana that are also easy to cook.

These recipes deliver two benefits—better health and satiating your sweet cravings. Bananas are naturally sweet so they don't need additional sugar to make a desserts, so they are the perfect sweet substitute.

Flourless Banana Dessert

Blend 1 chopped banana with 1 egg and 1 tbsp of cocoa powder (and some sugar if you want it sweeter) till it is smooth. Transfer to a cup and bake in an oven at 180 °C for 10–12 minutes. Eat out of the cup.

Banana Pancakes

Mix 1 cup of multigrain flour, a pinch of baking powder and a pinch of salt. Add 1 egg, some milk, a bit of honey, 10 gm butter or olive oil and whisk until the batter is smooth. Cook the pancakes on a pan that has been lightly greased with oil. Add thin slices of banana on top of the pancake before flipping it over. After a minute, flip it and cook for another 1 minute. Garnish with assorted cut fruits and serve.

Banana Snack

Marinate banana pieces in orange juice. Mix them with one of the following: unsweetened coconut, crushed peanuts or crushed cereal (quantity by choice) and serve.

Banana Ice Cream

Chop a ripe banana into small pieces and freeze in a Ziplock bag overnight. Next morning, blend it with 1 tbsp milk and a flavouring of your choice—cocoa, coffee, cinnamon, condensed milk, peanut butter or chopped nuts—till the mix is smooth. Transfer to a bowl and freeze for 1 hour. Dig in!

Cinnamon Banana

Chop a banana into thick circles and set them aside. Add 1 tbsp butter, 1 tbsp honey and a pinch of cinnamon powder to a pan, cook over low heat for 1 minute. Place the banana pieces in the pan and cook on both sides for 2–3 minutes till they caramelize. Sprinkle some sugar on top and serve hot. Pair with French toast if you like.

Coconut Banana

Make a slit lengthwise through the centre of a peeled banana. Whisk together 1 tbsp beaten cream and 1 tsp sugar. Stuff this mixture into the slit in the banana and sprinkle it with fresh or dry coconut flakes. Heat 1 tsp ghee in a pan, brown the banana on both sides and serve.

Banana Jam

Mash 2 bananas, mix in 2 tbsp of lemon juice, a few thinly chopped lemon rinds, ½ tsp cinnamon powder, a pinch of salt and 1 cup of sugar. Transfer to a pan and cook on high heat for 2 minutes till it begins to bubble, then cook on low heat for 15 more minutes, stirring occasionally. Let it cool, add 1 tsp of rum (optional) and pour into a glass jar. It will thicken as it cools.

Coffee and Banana Smoothie

Blend 1 sliced banana, 1 cup of low-fat milk, ½ cup of cold black coffee, 2 tsp sugar and ½ cup ice in a blender until smooth. Serve chilled.

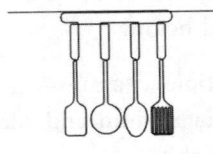

THIRTY

Summery Raw Mango

It is rare to find someone who doesn't love raw mango (*kachi kairi*). But not many know that it is extremely healthy too.

THE BENEFITS OF RAW MANGO

Raw mango is immensely beneficial for our health. Some of these benefits have been listed below.

- It delivers multiple vitamins—C, A, E—and minerals, like calcium, magnesium and niacin, that are brilliant for our heart health.
- It is really good for our digestion and helps keep constipation at bay.
- It is inherently cooling. So, it is just the food you should be having more of when the temperatures are rising.

STORY TIME

Madhumita Pyne, a Mumbai-based film-maker turned home chef and caterer, reports that raw mangoes are a staple in Bengali households during summer. 'We make chutneys with it, add it to dals, vegetable or fish curries. And every year, the moment it becomes available in the market, I make one of my favourite drinks ever—*aam pora sarbat*. It's a smoky version of *aam panna*. In olden days, when people used to cook in *unoon* or clay stoves, they would use the dying embers to roast the mangoes. These days, most people just do it on stove tops. I remember once my Maharashtrian house help saw the charred mangoes cooling on the kitchen counter, thought I had burned them by mistake and had thrown them away!' Madhumita shared.

Madhumita Pyne's Aam Pora Sarbat

'Roast raw mangoes till their skin is charred and the pulp is soft. Let them cool and remove their peels. Deseed and blend the pulp with sugar (I also use jaggery at times), some black salt and Bengali *bhaja masala* (dry roast and grind equal portions of whole cumin seeds, coriander seeds and dry chillies into a powder) along with water to make a thick paste.

'You can store this in a glass bottle in the fridge. To serve, add ice and cold water. Garnish with a pinch of the bhaja masala to add a punch.'

CHANGE HOW YOU COOK RAW MANGOES

There are many ways to have raw mangoes besides, of course, just biting into one or pickling it. Here are a few delicious raw mango recipes that are also easy to cook.

Aam ka Panna

Wash and boil 1 raw mango and let it cool. Peel, mash and strain the pulp. Whisk in 5 gm cumin powder, 2 crushed peppercorns, a pinch of hing, 8 tsp sugar and black salt to taste till the sugar has dissolved. Divide the mixture into glasses, fill them up with chilled water. Stir well and drink.

Raw Mango Chutney

Grind 250 gm chopped raw mangoes with 2 red chillies, a pinch of hing, 2 tbsp desiccated coconut, 2 tbsp jaggery and salt to taste into a coarse paste. Top with a tadka made in 1 tsp heated mustard oil with curry leaves and serve.

Raw Mango Curd Rice

In a pan, heat 1 tsp ghee. Add a pinch of mustard seeds, ½ tsp each of chana and urad dal, a pinch of hing and a few curry leaves. Then, add 2 chopped green chillies. Pour this tadka over a cup of cooked rice. Add 2 finely chopped raw mangoes to the rice. Finally, add ½ a cup of curd, salt to taste and mix well. Chill and eat.

Khatti Kairi Dal

Cook a cup of toor dal (you can also make this with chana dal) and mash it a little. Heat 2 tsp oil, add a pinch of mustard seeds, 2 chopped green chillies, 1 sliced raw mango, a pinch of turmeric, 1 tbsp jaggery and salt to taste. Cook for 5–7 minutes. Pour the cooked dal in and garnish with some grated ginger on top. Serve with rice.

Raw Mango Rice

Cook 1 cup of rice and set it aside. In 2 tsp heated oil, temper a pinch each of mustard and cumin seeds and hing, 2 dry red chillies, a few curry leaves and a few chopped cashews. Then, add 1 chopped raw mango and cook for some time. Mix or layer this preparation with the cooked rice. Pair with a raita and dig in.

Crunchy and Tangy Salad

Toss 2 chopped raw mangoes, 200 gm boiled chicken or prawns, 1 tbsp soaked *sabja* (basil) seeds, 2 tbsp roasted peanuts and 1 tbsp desiccated coconut in 1 tbsp mustard oil. Chill and serve.

Raw Mango Ambal

In 1 tbsp heated mustard oil, add 2 whole red chillies followed by a pinch of mustard seeds and 2 thinly sliced raw mangoes. Season with 2 tbsp sugar and salt to taste. Continue cooking and stirring till the sugar turns brownish. Add ½ a cup of water. Simmer for 10 minutes. Check seasonings and pair with roti.

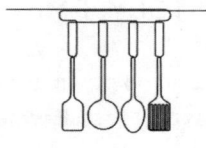

THIRTY ONE

Delicious Raw Papaya

There's a ton of information out there on the health benefits of papaya, and lots of people eat it for just these benefits. In terms of taste, it is an easily likeable fruit. However, not many know about the benefits of eating raw papaya, which is one of the most nutrient packed and versatile foods.

∽

STORY TIME

Sabyasachi Gorai, popularly known as Chef Saby Gorai, has always loved raw papaya. 'Most Bengali backyard gardens have at least 5 trees, out of which mango and papaya are the most common. Our garden was small, so there was no space for a mango tree but we definitely had a papaya tree. So, raw papaya was very much a part of my diet growing up. As a child, I would get excited to see the buds, followed by the flower and finally the fruit. We obviously cooked a lot with it too. 'I don't think any other community cooks mutton or chicken with papaya. However, Bengalis constantly innovate with raw papaya. My mother's raw papaya chutney, which we used to call plastic chutney, is something that really connects me to my childhood.

'To make it, thin slices of raw papaya are cooked in sugar

on low flame for a long time and it is called plastic because raw papaya becomes translucent or almost transparent once cooked. It was also used as *pepe raj chope chul*—a diet for someone with upset stomach. So, I started associating it with being sick, and, at some point, started detesting it and stopped eating it for a long time,' he recalled.

Much later in his career, Chef Saby suddenly landed up in Thailand and realized that raw papaya has many varieties and there are myriad ways to use and cook it. 'I remember I saw this lady on the street pounding a whole lot of spices, chillies, nuts, dried shrimp and finely shredded raw papaya in her cart—it looked beautiful. After that trip, I saw raw papaya with new eyes. In Bengal, I had never eaten raw papaya with peanuts and just fell in love with this combination. In fact, since my trip, Som Tam has been my most loved salad,' Chef Saby shared. Since then, he has used raw papaya in various forms to make fruit confit or shredded salad. 'I also use raw papaya in my restaurants as a tenderizer for cooking red meat and lamb and as marination. Or I mix it in kebabs to make them more juicy. So, it has been a fairly long journey for me with raw papaya from the time when I used to look down upon it to simply loving it and using it at every opportunity now. I think the only place in Delhi where you find good quality raw papaya even today is Chittaranjan Park because of the love Bengalis have for raw papaya,' he added.

THE BENEFITS OF RAW PAPAYA

Eating raw papayas has immense benefits. Some of them have been listed below.

- Raw papaya is a powerhouse of natural enzymes (a lot more than ripe papaya). The two power-packed enzymes in raw papaya are chymopapain and papain, which help breakdown protein, fats and carbohydrates.
- It helps promote digestive health and effectively cleanses our gut.
- It contains exceptional amounts of carotenoids (vitamin A), far more than carrots and tomatoes. The carotenoids found in raw papaya are more bioavailable (better absorbed). They are great for our eye health, skin health and immunity.
- It also helps reduce blood glucose levels by aiding the regeneration of beta cells and increasing insulin synthesis. So, it is a great food for diabetics.

CHANGE HOW YOU COOK RAW PAPAYA

The problem with raw papaya is that not many people know how to cook it. Here are a few delicious raw papaya recipes that are also easy to cook.

Papaya Juice, 2 Ways

- Blitz ½ a raw papaya, 1 cucumber and 1 beetroot. Add a dash of lemon, season with salt and pepper and sip. It's a perfect mid-morning drink.
- Blend raw papaya with a pinch of cardamom and salt and squeeze some lemon juice in it. Top with some sabja seeds that have been soaked for 2 hours and serve.

Raw Papaya Paratha

Grate and mix 1 raw papaya and radish. Season the mixture with spices of your choice, like red chilli powder and ajwain. Stuff this mixture in a whole wheat paratha. Cook on both sides, smear some ghee on top and serve. Pair with a grated carrot raita.

Roti Roll-Up

Spread a thick layer of spicy hummus on a roti and then roll it up with sliced, cold tandoori chicken (or sliced avocado) and slivers of cucumber, green chilli and raw papaya before serving.

Raw Papaya and Dal Sandwich

Take 2 slices of rye bread, spread thick, puréed dal (leftover dal cooked down on high heat can also work) on both slices. Top it with sliced tomatoes, boiled eggs, sliced boiled potatoes, lots of grated raw papaya and enjoy!

Raw Papaya Kachumbar

Mix slivers of raw papaya, carrots, green chillies and cucumber in equal quantities. Add some roasted, crushed peanuts, roasted melon seeds, salt and red chilli flakes to taste. Pour a dressing of olive oil, brown sugar, lemon juice and garlic over it and serve.

Fruit and Papaya Salad

In a large bowl, mix chopped pears or kiwis or apples (or a mix of these fruits), diced yellow and red bell peppers and slivered raw papaya. To make the dressing, mix lemon juice and zest, vinegar, sugar, coriander leaves, cumin powder and cinnamon powder. Pour gently over the salad. Chill and eat.

Raw Papaya Salad

Peel raw papaya and scrape out its seeds. Using a peeler, make thin, ribbon-like strips and place them a large bowl. Add chopped spring onions, fresh basil leaves and some coriander leaves. Whisk together olive oil, lime juice, honey and chilli flakes and drizzle this dressing over the salad. Finally, add peanuts and a handful of sprouts and toss. Chill and serve.

Som Tam Salad

Coarsely pound a few cloves of garlic, 2 red chillies, a few runner beans and cherry tomatoes together. Add 150 gm raw papaya and a few peanuts to this mixture and pound it again. Drizzle a dressing made by whisking together 1 tsp soy sauce, 1 tsp jaggery syrup and 1 tsp lemon juice on the salad. Garnish with some crushed peanuts and serve.

Quick Papaya Stir-Fry

Temper a pinch of methi and mustard seeds, a few curry leaves, 2 dry red chillies, sliced green chillies and a pinch of turmeric in 1 tbsp heated coconut oil. Sauté grated papaya in this mixture on sim for about 8–10 minutes, till it's cooked. Sprinkle salt to taste and 1 tbsp grated fresh or desiccated coconut on top, mix well and dig in.

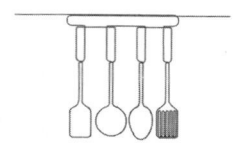

THIRTY TWO

Avocado: The Nutty Taste of Health

It is advisable to stick to locally available, regular and indigenous ingredients for everyday food preparations, simply because it is practical, pocket-friendly and good for our body. However, experimenting sometimes with some exotic foods (depending on availability and affordability) can bring some excitement and fun to our dull, everyday plates. Try adding avocados to your menu and score both on taste as well as health.

THE BENEFITS OF AVOCADO

Avocados are delicious. But not many know that they are a health bomb too. Some of the benefits of eating avocadoes have been listed below.

- This delicious fruit is loaded with health-promoting monounsaturated fatty acids, which are great for our heart; potassium, a mineral that helps regulate blood pressure; and the elusive folate, which is wonderful for heart health.
- It contains other disease-fighting compounds, such as lutein, beta-carotene and vitamin E.
- It also has a lot of gut healthy fibre.
- It greatly increases your body's ability to absorb the health-promoting carotenoids that vegetables provide.

CHANGE HOW YOU COOK AVOCADO

There are a lot of ways to use this unfamiliar fruit, which has now started making an appearance in India (one can only hope that it stays accessible and is priced right). In fact, it is an extremely versatile fruit. You can have it mashed, blended or sliced. The best news is that it does not need too much preparation and time to cook. Here are a few delicious avocado recipes that are also easy to cook.

Simple Sandwiches

Avocado and Balsamic Toast

Peel and deseed 1 avocado. Mash it in a small bowl with some salt, pepper and lemon juice (you can make this avocado mash in bulk and store it in the fridge to throw together a quick snack whenever you like). Top a toasted bread with the mashed avocado. Place 1 thinly sliced tomato over the avocado layer. Drizzle 1 tsp balsamic vinegar on top. Garnish with some red pepper flakes and a few basil leaves before serving.

Chickpeas and Avocado Toast

Mash ½ a cup of boiled chickpeas with salt, pepper and olive oil. Spread it over a toast. Mash ½ an avocado, add lemon juice, dried oregano or parsley. Spread it over the chickpea mixture. Top it with thin slices of red radish, cucumber or tomato and serve.

Hummus Avocado Toast

Spread 2 tbsp hummus on toast. Top with a sliced avocado. Season with salt, pepper and red chilli flakes to taste and serve.

Lemony Toast

Mash an avocado with a little lemon juice, spread it on toasted rye bread. Garnish with garlic salt, cumin, coriander, cardamom and white pepper powders to taste. Dig in!

Citrusy Toast

Combine 1 sliced avocado with oranges and fresh mint leaves. Spread this mixture on toasted rye bread, sprinkle it with garlic salt, cumin, coriander, cardamom and white pepper powders to taste (keep this seasoning mix ready in the fridge and use it as a common garnish) and serve.

Note: Replace the mayonnaise in sandwiches with avocado slices or ripe, mashed avocados. They pair well with chicken and turkey.

Summery Salads

Chickpeas, Feta and Avocado Salad

In a large mixing bowl, toss together a few torn pieces of romaine lettuce, 1 cup of boiled chickpeas, 1 chopped cucumber, a few sliced olives and 2 green onions. In a small bowl, whisk together 1 tbsp olive oil, 1 tbsp vinegar, a few chopped garlic pods, 1 tsp mustard sauce, salt and pepper to taste. Pour the dressing over the salad and mix thoroughly until the ingredients are well-coated. Add a sliced avocado, 50 gm feta cheese and herbs of your choice on top and toss gently before serving.

Avocado Chicken Salad

In a bowl, mix ½ cup of Greek yoghurt or cream cheese, 1 tbsp mustard sauce and 1 tbsp vinegar. Add oregano, salt and pepper to taste. Fold in 100 gm smoked or boiled chicken cut into small chunks, 1 sliced red pepper, ¼ cup of corn kernels and 1 sliced avocado. Place in lettuce cups and serve.

Avocado Rajma Power Bowl

Mix ½ cup cooked rajma, ½ a sliced onion, bell pepper, tomato and cucumber, 1 chopped green chilli, ¼ cup sweet corn and 1 cup sliced avocado. Add some chopped fresh mint and basil leaves. For the dressing, whisk together 1 tbsp olive oil, ½ tbsp lemon juice, 2 crushed garlic cloves, oregano, salt and black pepper to taste. Drizzle this over the salad and serve.

Avocado and Orange Salad

Combine 1 sliced avocado with 1 orange and a bunch of fresh mint leaves. Season with salt and oregano and dig in.

Note: Tossing a few slices of avocado in your colorful salad, or mixing some chopped avocado into your favourite salsa will not only add a rich, creamy flavour but will also greatly increase your body's ability to absorb the health-promoting carotenoids that vegetables provide. Furthermore, avocado helps deliver vitamin A, which is a fat soluble vitamin.

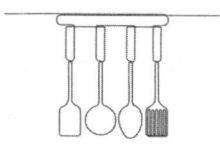

Part 6

Healthy Sweets

Anyone who has a sweet tooth craves dessert to end their meals. Why not make the ending to our meal not just sweet but healthy too? It helps to make your own desserts because when we make or bake our own treats, we can alter them according to our taste preferences or health needs. Most importantly, we can restrict the amount of sugar and fats in home-cooked sweets.

Today, it is widely accepted that balancing all 5 tastes—salty, sweet, sour, bitter and umami—is the key to satisfaction and good health. According to Ayurveda, too, consuming food that has a proper balance of all tastes is essential to nourish the body and stay healthy. Of course, when consumed in excess, sweets can lead to insulin resistance and diabetes.

So, going back to the traditional way of making your own desserts, even if in small batches at home, is a smart tactic.

THIRTY THREE

Halwa Happiness

There is something about halwa that brings a smile on everyone's face. It is a comfort food that has been part of everyone's joy-giving rituals growing up. It is often made during festivals for the simple reason that it is universally liked. Are you craving halwa? Why not try something different and surprise your family?

Chickoo Halwa

Peel and pulp 4 *chickoos* (sapodilla fruits). Pour the chickoo pulp into a pan. Add ½ a cup of milk and boil it, stirring constantly. When it thickens, add 80 gm khoya and continue stirring as it cooks. Add 1 tbsp sugar and ½ tbsp ghee. Cook on low heat for 2–4 more minutes, stirring the mixture constantly. Take off heat and let it cool a bit. Garnish with almonds and serve hot.

Coconut Halwa

Soak ½ a cup of rice in water for 2–3 hours. Grind the soaked rice and 2 cups of grated fresh coconut with some water until it turns into a fine paste and set it aside.

In a pan, bring ½ a cup of sugar and ½ a cup of water to a boil till it thickens. Add a pinch of cardamom powder and the coconut—rice paste. Keep stirring till it thickens and starts sticking to the sides of the pan. Just before turning off the flame, add 1 tbsp ghee and mix well. Garnish with some chopped cashew and raisins before serving.

Safed Kaddu Halwa

Coarsely grate 1 cup white pumpkin (*safed kaddu*) and drain the excess moisture in it by squeezing it in a cloth. Add it to a pot with 2 cups of milk and ¾ cup sugar. Cook over low heat till the mixture becomes soft while stirring constantly. Add ½ a cup of ghee and cook till the ghee separates. Stir in cardamom powder and cashew nuts to taste. Spread the mixture in a greased tray and let it cool for 30 minutes. Cut into squares and serve.

Gluten-Free Baked Halwa

Mix ¼ cup of cream with a pinch of cinnamon and set it aside. Whisk ½ a cup of butter with ½ a cup of sugar. Then, add 1 tsp cornflour to it. Whisk the cream into the butter. Add some slivered almonds and mix gently. Pour this into a buttered pan. Bake in preheated oven at 200 °C for 45 minutes. Meanwhile, make a syrup by boiling 1 cup of sugar, 1.5 cups of water, 1 stick of cinnamon and 2 whole cloves for 10 minutes. Take out the cinnamon and cloves. Pour the syrup over the hot halwa. Cool and serve.

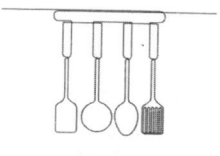

THIRTY FOUR

Fruits Make Perfect Desserts

We must all eat more fruits. They are the best way to ensure that we get multiple antioxidants and essential minerals and vitamins that our body needs, along with the necessary fibre for our gut.

One underrated and lesser-known use of fruits is that they make perfect desserts with just a little effort. They are fabulous replacements for those high calorie, trans fat- and preservatives-laden heavy desserts. Fruits are naturally sweet so they help cut down sweet cravings. If you simply add 2–3 fruits in your daily diet, you'll feel the difference within a few days.

STORY TIME

Subha J. Rao, Mangalore-based journalist and founder of Made In Mangalore By Subha (madeinmangalore.in), is a fruit lover. She recalled that during her years working in Coimbatore, a journalist colleague and friend often brought a dessert for lunch and one of her favourites was sliced apples with raisins and honey dressed in curd. 'Just before serving it, she would crush some toasted walnuts on top. None of these desserts took up much time to put together, but they livened up the office lunch hour, offered us companionship and a promise of something to look forward to. I still remember its delicious taste,' Subha added.

∽

CHANGE HOW YOU COOK FRUIT DESSERTS

Here are a few tricks to satisfy your sweet cravings in a smart and easy way using fruits.

- Drizzle a bit of honey over mixed watermelon and muskmelon balls.
- Blend bananas and strawberries, freeze into cubes and eat as an ice cream.
- Sauté ½ a banana for a minute or so and sprinkle with 1 tbsp chopped nuts and a drizzle of caramelized sugar.
- Before you bite into a pear or apple, sprinkle it with a bit of honey and any roasted seeds to make it more filling and crunchy.
- Pair chopped apples with some feta cheese and raisins or prunes.
- Grill grapes or a banana. They taste great once caramelized.
- Wash and freeze any whole soft fruit, like mangoes or peaches. Then, cut it into large pieces, top with chocolate or raspberry syrup and a small dollop of ice cream.

Here are a few delicious fruits-based dessert recipes that are also easy to cook.

Mango Tango

Blend 2 mangoes, 1 banana, 1 cup of curd, 2 tsp honey, 6 ice cubes and 1 tsp vanilla extract until smooth. Refrigerate for 3 hours. Dig in.

Apple, 2 Ways

- **Apple crunch:** Peel and grate 2 apples. Spread the grated apple on a baking dish and sprinkle it with 2 tsp sugar, 2 tsp roasted, popped amaranth and a pinch of cinnamon powder. Bake in an oven at 180 °C for 5–6 minutes or till the apples are done. Take out of the over and serve.
- **Stuffed apple:** Bake an apple stuffed with raisins and sprinkled with cinnamon at 200 °C for 30 minutes. Top it with ¼ cup of fat-free vanilla yoghurt and serve.

Litchi Dessert

Deseed 200 gm litchis. Mix lightly sweetened honey or sugar and 100 gm *chena* (crumbled cottage cheese). Stuff this into the litchis. Chill and serve.

Fruity Delight

Blend 100 gm cottage cheese with 2 tbsp sugar, 3 tbsp milk and a drizzle of vanilla essence into a paste. Place 1 bowl of (any) mixed fruits cut into small pieces in a bowl. Pour the paste over the fruit mixture and toss it together gently. Chill and serve.

Pineapple and Paneer

Blend 100 gm crushed pineapple pieces with 100 gm cottage cheese. Spread this on toast and serve.

Candied Orange Peels

Make a sugar syrup from 2 cups of water and ½ a cup of sugar. Bring it to a boil and add orange rinds. Boil for 30 minutes and remove from heat. Place on wax paper and let it dry before serving.

Stewed Fruit

Quarter any fruit (pears would be great) and sprinkle cinnamon and nutmeg powder over it. Add fresh ginger and some jaggery or honey to it. Place the mixture in a pan with just enough water to cover the fruit. Bring to a boil and simmer covered for about 15 minutes, stirring occasionally. Eat as is or mixed with some yoghurt or granola.

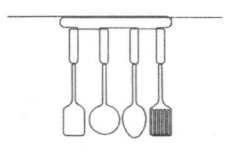

THIRTY FIVE

Delicious Home-Made Laddoos

Who doesn't love *laddoos*? They are delicious and people usually have lovely memories of them.

STORY TIME

Nishant Choubey, a celebrated chef, is particularly fond of amaranth. He shared a golden memory from his childhood. He said that now he cannot go back to stealing *amaranth ke laddoo* from his grandmother's hidden pot, but just reliving that memory makes this laddoo special for him. 'She would always count them before hiding them. However, she would invariably forget the number and point towards me as the culprit. I would act innocent and suggest that our pet had taken them away. I used to love them so much,' he chuckled while reminiscing. Nishant's grandmother had a special recipe for amaranth laddoos with amaranth, jaggery and nuts.

Chef Nishant's Amaranth Laddoo

Heat 2 tbsp ghee and roast 1 cup of makhana in it. Heat 1 tbsp ghee in another pan and add 1 cup of grated or powdered jaggery to it. Pour in a little bit of water and cook till the jaggery melts. Add 2 cups of popped amaranth and makhana to the jaggery syrup, mix well and cook for 1 minute. Take it off the flame and add ¼ tsp cardamom powder and a pinch of saffron (you can also add a little bit of chilli powder, but this is optional) and mix well Ensure that your hands are wet and start shaping the hot mixture into laddoos. Allow the laddoos to cool down, then store in an airtight container.

CHANGE HOW YOU COOK LADDOOS

Here are a few healthy, delicious home-made laddoo recipes that are also easy to make.

Besan ke Laddoo

Roast 500 gm besan in 300 gm ghee on low heat till it turns light golden in colour. Then, add 750 gm sugar to it and cook for ½ a minute. Take the mixture off the heat, add crushed pistachios and almonds and mix. While the mixture is still warm, shape into laddoos. Store in an airtight container once they have cooled.

Sattu ke Laddoo

Lightly roast 500 gm sattu with 500 gm jaggery. Transfer this mixture onto a large plate. Add cardamom powder, finely chopped cashews and pistachios. Knead and shape into laddoos, adding coconut milk as required.

Malai Laddoo

To ¼ cup of heated ghee, add 1 cup suji and roast for about 5 minutes till it is light brown. Add 3 tbsp of desiccated coconut and briefly roast for 2 minutes. Add nuts, like almonds, cashews, pistachios, and roast for 2 more minutes. Whisk together ¼ cup heavy cream, 1 cup powdered sugar and a pinch of cardamom powder. Pour this mixture into the suji–coconut mix. While the mixture is still warm, shape it into medium-sized laddoos.

Date and Oatmeal Laddoos

Cook 100 gm dates in 100 ml fresh orange juice on low heat until the mixture reaches the consistency of a mash and allow it to cool. In a separate bowl, mix 100 gm oats, 1 tbsp honey and 1 tbsp pistachios. Fold this mixture into the cooled dates. Spread the mixture evenly on a tray greased with ghee. Shape into laddoos while it is still warm.

Peanut Laddoos

In 250 ml water, add 250 gm jaggery and boil till a thick syrup forms. Stir in ½ cup of roasted peanuts, 1 cup of cooked rice, a pinch of cardamom powder and ½ cup of dry coconut flakes. Top it off with a little bit of ghee. Let the mixture cool a bit and then gently roll into laddoos.

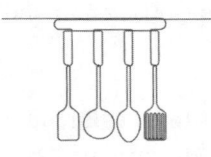

THIRTY SIXTH

Smart Summer Desserts

Who doesn't like desserts? However, ready-made desserts can be packed with a lot of additives, food colouring, preservatives, besides packing a humongous number of calories. This is enough to scare those who are health-conscious or can at least make us feel terribly guilty. So, should one stop eating desserts totally?

No, there is no need to go cold turkey. The fact is that the more you try to run away from sweets, the more you'll think about and crave them. Instead, what you really need to do is start making healthy and tasty desserts at home to get your sweet fix responsibly. This way you will be able to control the calorie count and make sure you sneak in some healthy ingredients that are good for you. Indulge in these non-guilty pleasures that are low in calories, super high in satisfaction and easy to make.

Unsweet Sweet

Cut carrots into small batons, lightly glaze them with honey or maple syrup and roll them in grated coconut. Enjoy this as an after-dinner dessert. It tastes quite like *gajar ka halwa*, especially if you add some chopped nuts and raisins, but it is so much better for our teeth. It also delivers more nutrition than regular desserts!

Tall Fruit Sundae

Layer the following elements on top of one another in a sundae glass: 1 scoop of flavoured frozen yoghurt, 1 scoop of no-sugar sorbet, different diced fruits of your choice—like mangoes, melons, strawberries, etc.—and some muesli. Top this off with any blended fruit as a stand-in for a sauce, an indulgent splash of low-fat cream and dark chocolate chips. Serve chilled.

This sundae might look humongous but it only has approximately 200 calories. What's more, the fruits hydrate us and provide antioxidants and the curd delivers protein along with loads of satisfaction and colour that makes children love this dessert.

Perfect Paneer Dessert

Whisk 100 gm mashed paneer and 20 gm jaggery with 50 gm of ground and soaked almonds. Flatten onto a dish and sprinkle 2 tbsp chopped pistachios on top. Refrigerate for 3 hours before digging in.

Walnut Delight

Mix 8 crushed walnuts and 4 deseeded, chopped dates with 1 cup of beaten curd. Drizzle 1 tbsp pure maple syrup on top. Chill and serve.

Healthy Parfait

Layer chilled curd, 1 sliced, preferably red-coloured, fruit—like strawberries, pomegranate, deseeded red grapes, dried cranberries etc.—and crunchy, roasted flaxseeds. Top with roasted walnuts and dig in. This makes for the perfect breakfast treat.

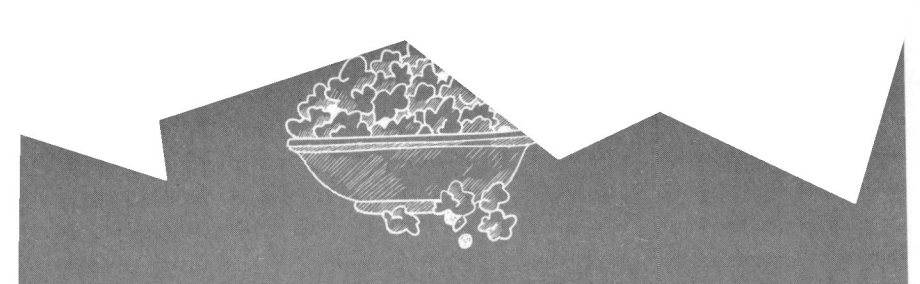

Part 7

Snack Attack

Snacking involves eating food or drinks between your main meals. It is often equated with having high-calorie, processed foods, like chips or cookies. Regardless of this popular definition, I would urge you to have snacks and not feel guilty about it.

Snacking is not as bad as it is made out to be nowadays. Rather, it can make you less cranky, provide essential nutrients and help control your appetite. This does not mean that I am green lighting all snacks, particularly ones that can be bad for our health and make us put on weight, like deep-fried foods.

However, not all snacks are bad. I have 3 golden rules for snacking right:

- always be prepared with healthy snacking options;
- work healthy snacks into your diet;
- include snacks in your food plan for the day.

If you don't have something healthy handy, you are likely to grab the first, potentially unhealthy, thing that's around. So, it is important to plan ahead of time and keep some healthy snacks, like nuts, within reach. Arm yourself with the right snacks for the inevitable 5 p.m. snack craving. After all, the gap between lunch and dinner tends to be long and can tempt us to eat junk food.

Snacking does not necessarily have to be unhealthy. You can snack the right way. Read on to know how.

THIRTY SEVEN

Power Snacks for Your Workstation

At 11.00 a.m., your stomach starts growling and you start looking around for something to munch. Cut to 5.00 p.m., it's the same story again. So, what's the solution? How can you stop yourself from eating unhealthy snack at these times?

You don't have to stop yourself but just know that the key words here are 'the right snacks'. So, to make sure you eat something right, keep it close at hand. Yes, right in your desk drawer or in the nearby office fridge.

Here are a few healthy snack ideas that are also easy to make.

Fruit Power

Try to have at least one to two fruits during your work hours. They are the perfect snack because the fructose in them gives you a quick energy boost. Keep finger fruits, like oranges, guava, apples etc., handy. If you have access to a fridge, then an airtight container full of cut and chilled papaya or watermelon can be great too. Grab a different fruit every day (change it with the seasons) and try to pair it with a little protein (low-fat cheese, curd or peanut butter) to boost its satiety value.

Eggy Delight

Take a hard-boiled egg with you to work every day and have it when you need a quick pick-me-up. It's a perfectly satisfying snack and is high in protein, so it helps curb hunger. Have it with salt, pepper or mustard. You can even make it an egg salad by simply chopping up 1 egg and mixing it with 1 tbsp low-fat mayonnaise and some sunflower or flaxseeds.

Favourite Cracker

Crackers and cheese or peanut butter is a snack that always works. The combination of complex carbohydrates and protein helps stabilize blood sugar and leaves you feeling full for longer. You could also try pairing crackers with apple butter, hummus or salsa.

Perk Up Food

Feeling really grumpy? Eating cold-water fish, such as salmon, tuna or sardines, may help. In fact, they are the perfect snack between meetings. The antioxidants and omega-3 fatty acids (good fats) in them can enhance cognitive function. So, keep tins of these fish handy if you want to stay in a good mood. If you are a vegetarian, baked beans are a good option.

Go Nuts!

Often, a combination of nuts and dry fruits works best as a snack—both in terms of taste and health. Keep combinations like almonds and dates or apricots, walnuts and raisins in airtight containers or zipper bags so that you can grab them easily and snack. It is better than chips any day! Nuts are a filling food thanks to their protein content. They are also a good way to have some healthy fats. However, make sure you choose dry-roasted and unsalted varieties.

Need for Seed

Like nuts, seeds—like flaxseed and sunflower—are a good snack, as they contain heart-healthy fats, magnesium, fibre and potassium. Just don't have too many, as nuts and seeds are high-calorie foods. A healthy snack serving is about 2 tbsp. Again, you must pick dry-roasted, unsalted seeds.

Get Chocolate Cheer

Keep some chocolate handy to tide you over really low times at work. Chocolate, especially the dark variety (70 percent cocoa or higher), has many health benefits. It is loaded with antioxidants but because it is high in calories, reach for chocolate in moderation—have only 2 or 3 small squares of dark chocolate occasionally.

A Quick Snack

Boil 30 gm masoor dal in 1 cup vegetable or chicken stock. Add a few chopped spring onions or spinach leaves and cook until it is a dry, spreadable consistency. Spread on a toast and eat.

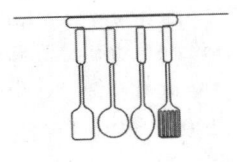

THIRTY EIGHT

Easy-Peasy Chai Snacks

At 11.00 a.m. or 4.00 p.m., you begin fidgeting in your seat, but it's not really your stomach but your mind that is growling, asking for something to munch on. So, you reach out for that laddoo that came from someone's puja, adding up to a whooping 200 odd calories to your daily diet. Then, you go make some Maggi or open that packet of chips you had hidden (obviously not well enough).

There are 3 main reasons you feel hungry between meals: you skipped breakfast or lunch; your meals were not satisfying; or you are simply bored because there is a lull at work or someone else around you is snacking so you also mindlessly munch.

Figuring out why you snack is the first step to curbing it. The second step is to choose the right snacking options. There are many healthy and tasty options available. Ensure they are always available to you so that you reach for them instead of the usual unhealthy options. Don't think of snacks as extras. Instead, consciously work healthy ones into your diet and make them a part of your food plan for the day. Print out a list of healthy snack options and keep it handy at your desk along with the information about where they can be sourced from so that when the craving strikes, you know what to order.

When snacking, portion size is of utmost importance. So, just by cutting down the amount that you are eating, you can keep things under control. Snacking is not bad. It doesn't inherently make you gain weight; only too many calories do that. In fact, the right kind of snacking can actually help increase your metabolic rate and stimulate your body to burn more fat and fill in the nutritional gaps in your diet. All you need to do is to get smart about it. Time to say no to samosas, muffins, chips, bread pakora and instant noodles. Instead, opt for these easy and quick recipes.

Corn, 2 Ways

- **Kurkure baby corn:** Slit a handful of baby corn into 2 parts and blanched them. Heat 1 tbsp oil and sauté the baby corn in it for 2 minutes on medium flame. Sprinkle ¼ tsp chilli flakes, ½ tsp vinegar and salt to taste and sauté for 2 minutes. Garnish with oregano and serve hot.
- **Masala corn:** Microwave frozen corn for 2 minutes. Season it with some salt and pepper and dig in. It just takes 3–4 minutes to prepare this snack but it's healthy and yummy. If you have a sweet tooth, drizzle the corn with some maple syrup or honey instead of salt and pepper.

Peas Chaat

To 1 cup of boiled peas, add ½ a cup each of chopped onion and tomatoes and a few chopped green chillies. Squeeze 2 tbsp lemon juice on top, sprinkle salt, pepper and amchoor or chaat masala to taste and serve.

Makhana, 2 Ways

- **Murmure and makhana magic:** Toss ½ cup of puffed rice and ½ cup of roasted makhana with 1 boiled and cubed potato, ½ a chopped onion and tomato each. Sprinkle some herbs or spices to taste, mix and serve.
- **Makhana bhelpuri:** To 1 cup of roasted makhana, add 1

chopped onion, cucumber and tomato each. Season with black salt and a generous squeeze of lemon. Mix and serve.

Desi Chaat

Chop 1 boiled potato into small cubes. Toss in 1 tbsp crushed chivda and ½ a roasted papad, 1 tbsp roasted chana, 1 tsp tamarind sauce, 2 tbsp curd, 3 tbsp green moong dal or kala chana sprouts, 2 tbsp pomegranate seeds and 1 chopped cucumber. Mix well and serve.

Feta and Apple Bowl

Chop an apple and crumble some feta cheese, a few roasted, crushed makhana and 1 tbsp of roasted flaxseeds on top. Mix and dig in.

Sprouts, 5 Ways

- **Sprouts mix:** On a bed of lettuce, place 1 chopped beetroot, 2 tbsp bean sprouts, 1 carrot cut into sticks, 1 tbsp crumbled feta (or any other soft cheese, like goat cheese) and 1 tbsp roasted peanuts. Season with salt, pepper and herbs of your choice, mix and dig in.
- **Sprouted pulses with Indian garnishes:** Take 1 cup of raw or sprouted moong, masoor or other dals. Sprinkle a little chivda or sev on them. Sprinkle a pinch of salt and chaat masala, toss together and serve.
- **Dressed sprouts:** Mix ½ cup each of chopped and boiled broccoli with carrots and mixed sprouts (chana, moong, Brussel). Blend a few mint leaves, 2–3 cloves garlic and 1 tbsp olive oil in the food processor, pour over the sprouts mixture and serve.
- **Sprouts delight:** To heated oil, add a pinch each of mustard seeds, cumin seeds, 1 slit green chilli and a little hing, in this

order. Then, immediately throw in 100 gm sprouts (any dal sprouts you have handy) and stir-fry for about 2 minutes. Add ¼ tsp sugar and stir for another 15 seconds. Turn off the heat. Add 1 tsp lime juice and salt to taste. Season with chopped coriander leaves when it is still hot and serve.

- **Sprouts and roots salad:** In a bowl, add 1 cup of any lentil sprouts, 1 boiled and diced potato, 1 shredded carrot, 1 small sliced onion, 1 small bunch of fresh and chopped coriander leaves, ½ a diced radish and 2 sliced green chillies. Whisk together 1 cup of hung curd with salt and pepper to taste. Pour it over the sprouts mix and toss well. Lay out a layer of lettuce on a platter and spoon the salad over it.

Quick Cheese Balls

Wet 2 slices of bread in a little water and squeeze the water out. Break the damp bread to small pieces and put them on a plate. Add 30 gm grated cheese, ½ a chopped onion, 2 chopped green chillies, a few coriander leaves and salt to taste to the bread pieces. Mix all the ingredients well so that the mixture resembles a dough. Roll into equal-sized balls. Air- or deep-fry and serve hot with ketchup or chutney.

Crackers, 2 Ways

- **Cracker delight:** On a cheese cracker, spread some cream cheese, a finely chopped mixture of red and yellow peppers, spring onions and garlic. Season with some pepper and enjoy.
- **Walnut magic:** Blend ½ cup of walnuts, 1 cup hung curd, a few sprigs of mint leaves and coriander leaves, a few chopped cloves of garlic, salt and pepper to taste into a paste. Spread on a toasted bread or cracker and eat.

Fragrant Moong Bean and Vegetable Toss

Soak ½ cup of moong beans overnight in fresh water. Cook them by boiling for some time, strain and set them aside. Heat 1 tbsp olive oil in a frying pan over medium heat. Add ½ tsp each of the cracked cumin, coriander and fennel seeds. Cook while stirring frequently. When the seeds start to pop, take off the heat and pour the oil on top of the moong beans. Toss in 2 chopped cloves garlic, 2 tbsp vinegar, ½ tsp chilli flakes and ½ tsp of salt. Stir to combine and set aside.

Add some steamed carrot and French beans (and any other vegetable you like) to the moong beans. Squeeze lemon juice on top and serve.

Carrot Sticks

Slice carrots into ¼ inch thick sticks and steam or microwave them for 5 minutes. Stir in 1 tbsp maple syrup and 1 tbsp Dijon mustard while the carrots are hot. Dig in.

Raw Banana Cutlets

Pressure cook 2 raw bananas. Once they have cooled, peel and mash them. Season with ½ tsp red chilli powder, 1 tsp lemon juice, some chopped coriander leaves, 1 tsp coriander powder and ½ tsp garam masala and mix well. Divide the mixture into equal portions and make small cutlets, roll in some besan and cook in an oiled pan till they are golden brown on both sides. Serve with green coriander chutney.

Spicy Snacky Paneer

Make a paste with ginger, garlic, curd, salt, pepper, a little oil and turmeric. Marinate cubes of 200 gm paneer in this paste for 1 hour. Place these cubes in the oven and roast for 15 minutes at 200 °C. When they are done, place them on a bed of lettuce or baby spinach, sprinkle herbs of your choice on top and serve.

Raw Banana Fry

Wash, peel and cut 200 gm raw banana into long slices. Marinate in a mixture of 1 tbsp ginger garlic and chilli pastes each, 1 tsp turmeric, 2 tbsp red chilli powder, salt to taste and 1 tbsp lemon juice for 30 minutes. Coat in a mixture of 75 per cent rice flour and 25 per cent suji and pan-fry in any oil of your choice till golden brown. Serve hot!

Gujarati Pudla

Mix ½ cup besan, ½ cup of any grated seasonal vegetables (peas, bottle gourd, spinach, methi leaves, green peppers, etc.), some ginger, a few coriander leaves, ½ cup curd and salt and red chilli powder to taste. Add some water to this mixture until it reaches a pourable consistency. Cook it on a pan like an omelette with minimal oil. Enjoy this savoury, soft and thin pancake.

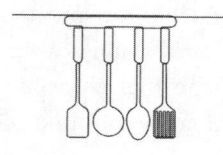

THIRTY NINE

Chip-Chip Hooray!

Most of the health issues we face today are caused by the fact that we now prioritize comfort and convenience over everything else and that taste has become a sort of non-negotiable factor in our food. So, we eat packaged comfort foods with a vengeance, turning a blind eye to the fact that the more processed food we eat, the worse off our health is because the ingredients in such foods are often suspect.

In fact, wrong snacking hinders sustainable weight loss. The biggest culprits here, according to me, are the omnipresent and accessible potato chips. I realized early on in my practice that potato chips are a formidable foe and that weaning people off their satisfying crunch can be quite a task, even though most people, I believe, are aware that chips are loaded with calories and excess fat. Usually, there are around 350 calories and 30 gm fat in every 100 gm of chips.

So, I changed strategies and decided to just get rid of the baddies (preservatives, excess sodium, additives, unsafe colour and so on) but keep the crunch and taste. I have helped my clients swap packets of chips with home-made, equally delicious and extremely healthy baked chip options and the experiment has succeeded!

Here are 2 delicious recipes that are both healthy and easy to make.

Sweet Potato Chips

Cut 100 gm sweet potatoes into very thin slices. In a large bowl, toss them with 1 tbsp oil, ½ tsp sea salt and pepper to taste. Now place them in a single layer on an un-greased baking sheet. Preheat the oven to 200 °C and bake the sweet potatoes for 10–15 minutes while looking out for browning. Rotate the baking sheet once until the edges are crisp but the sweet potatoes are still soft in the centre. Let them cool completely until they are crisp before digging in.

Note: Not only are these chips delicious but they might also help you get a little saner in today's stress-ridden times. Sweet potatoes are a great source of the magnesium, which is known as a relaxing and anti-stress mineral.

Baked Beetroot Chips

Preheat the oven to 200 °C. Clean 100 gm beetroots and slice them thinly. Put an oven wire rack on top of a baking sheet. If you don't have one, brush your baking sheet with about 1 tsp olive oil and arrange the beetroots on it. Before putting them in the oven, brush the beetroots with 1 tsp olive oil, salt and pepper to taste on both sides. Put them in oven and bake for 15 minutes, then turn the beetroots over and cook for another 15–20 minutes. Take them out. Let them cool and get crispy.

Note: The nitrates in beetroot help lower blood pressure and fight heart diseases too.

MIND THE SAUCES TOO

To go with these healthy chips, forget sugar- and salt-laden ketchups and fancy sauces, try these healthy home-made dips instead.

Salsa Verde Dip (Green Tomato Dip)

Place 2 green tomatoes and 2 jalapeños in a pot of water. Bring to a boil and cook until the tomatoes and jalapeños are slightly soft. Add them to a blender along with ½ an onion, 3 tbsp lime juice, salt, black pepper to taste and ½ a cup of fresh cilantro or coriander leaves. Purée to a desired consistency and refrigerate.

Fresh Tomato Salsa Dip

In a bowl, combine 2 chopped tomatoes, ½ a finely chopped onion, 1 finely chopped jalapeño, 1 tsp lemon juice, ½ a cup of finely chopped cilantro, salt and pepper to taste, a pinch of dry oregano or cumin powder and 1 tsp sugar. Refrigerate this mixture for 30 minutes before serving.

Peas Dip

Purée 1 cup of boiled peas and mix it with ½ a cup of curd, black pepper and salt to taste, 2 chopped green chillies and 1 tbsp lemon juice to make a healthy dip.

Nutty Dip

Take ½ a cup of walnuts, 1 cup of hung curd, a few sprigs of mint and coriander leaves, a couple of garlic cloves and salt and pepper to taste. Blend all the ingredients into a paste and serve.

Green Dip

Boil and finely chop 200 gm spinach and mix it in 1 cup of thick curd. Temper the mixture with ½ tsp of mustard seeds and 2 green chillies.

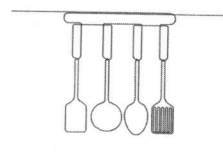

Part 8

The Bonus Section

Every meal we eat has a bearing on our body and health, which is why every bite counts. Making healthy eating an intrinsic part of our lifestyle is the way to go.

Regardless of your age, whether you stay with family or alone, if you have the time or inclination to cook, how busy and stressed you may be, if you have the time to experiment in the kitchen and whether you are a passionate foodie or agnostic to food, you should make all your food-related decisions by prioritizing your health and nutritional needs.

In this section, I have provided detailed recipes for healthy and tasty breakfasts, lunches, accompaniments, like chutneys and pickles, salads, sandwiches and more.

From rainy-days to heart-healthy foods, there is a recipe for everyone here.

FORTY

Breakfast for Singles

You have probably heard the advice, 'Start your day right to have a great day ahead' umpteen times. What that means in nutritional terms is to begin the day with a tasty breakfast that gives us all the essential nutrients and leaves us satisfied and happy. This is even more important today when we are working from home and unable to blur the lines between work and leisure. A good breakfast can start you off on the right foot to take on the never-ending demands on your time and energy during the course of the day.

TIPS FOR A NUTRITIOUS BREAKFAST

- Include at least one fruit or vegetable, preferably one that is rich in vitamin C, such as oranges, grapes, melons or amla.
- Include a good source of fibre (at least 3 gm fibre per serving). This includes foods like a whole wheat chapatti, whole grain breads, whole grain cereals (bran, oatmeal, daliya, shredded wheat), brown rice, fruits and vegetables.
- Include a good source of protein, like milk, soy milk, cheese, curd, meat, fish, poultry, beans or eggs.
- Include a bit of fat, like nuts and seeds.

Here are some delicious breakfast recipes that are also easy to make at home.

Bread Breakfast, 3 Ways

- Mash ½ cup boiled rajma or lobia beans and mix them with 2 tbsp curd. Add mustard, dill, parsley or pepper to taste. Spread this mixture on a multigrain bread. Top with lettuce, ½ each of a sliced cucumber and tomato. Chill and serve.
- Lightly toast 2 slices of whole wheat bread, spread a thin layer of low-fat cheese spread, some mustard and chilli sauces. Top it with 1 sliced tomato and sprinkle some black pepper and torn-up basil leaves. Grill the sandwich till the tomatoes have softened. If you are not calorie-conscious, you can add some grated cheese as well.
- Sauté 1 clove of garlic in 2 tsp heated olive oil until it is aromatic. Add 100 gm mushrooms, chopped roughly. Cook them till their moisture evaporates. Season with salt, pepper, lemon juice and dried oregano or any other preferred herb. Place the cooked mushrooms onto whole wheat toast. Pair with a fruit and choose a drink to go with this breakfast, be it green tea, vegetable juice or fresh coconut water.

Breakfast Cheelas

Soak ½ cup of whole moong for 1 hour. Then, grind the moong with green chillies and 1 clove of garlic (optional). Add salt, ½ tsp each of fennel seeds and red chilli powder. Add water to make a thick but spreadable batter. Smear a hot, flat bottomed tawa with a little oil. To make the tawa non-stick, rub a sliver of cut onion across it. Spread the batter on the tawa in the shape of a cheela. Cook till both sides are lightly brown, adding just a little oil to let it cook. Serve hot. Pair this with a glass of juice or buttermilk for a protein-rich start to your day.

Fibre-Rich Parathas

For a filling breakfast, try the traditional stuffed paratha but make it healthy and low-fat. Make the dough by kneading 50 per cent whole wheat flour, 50 per cent bran and ½ tsp ajwain. Stuff the paratha with any leftovers—keema, vegetables, boiled potatoes, mashed and seasoned. Add fresh or dried methi leaves to the dough for an exciting flavour. Cook on a non-stick tawa and smear with ghee once cooked. Serve with a kachumbar salad. To make this, mix 1 each of a small, finely chopped onion and tomato with plenty of fresh coriander leaves. Season with lemon juice, salt and sugar. Pair with a glass of buttermilk seasoned with roasted ground cumin powder and black pepper.

Bean Salad

Steam a handful of French beans and a handful each of sprouted chana, rajma and kala chana. Dice 1 small cucumber, 1 small boiled potato and 1 small apple. Mix all these ingredients in a large bowl along with a fistful of raisins. Squeeze lemon juice over the salad.

For the dressing, whisk together 1 tbsp olive oil, the juice of 1 lemon, 1 tsp vinegar, a dash of mustard and 1 clove of crushed garlic. Let the dressing sit for a while to allow the flavours to infuse before pouring it over the salad.

Tear up a few leaves of fresh lettuce, wash well, pat dry and add to the rest of the ingredients just before you eat. For a variation, you can add a boiled egg. Pair this with a yoghurt and apple smoothie.

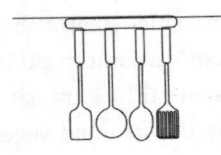

FORTY ONE

Jazz Up Your Breakfast: Go Regional

Bored of the ubiquitous western breakfast of toast and egg, oats with milk and even the regular stuff you eat day in and out, like poha or upma? It's time to jazz up your breakfast with some regional flavours. Try these dishes from across the country and make your mornings happier, brighter and, of course, healthier. After all, eating diversely is an important tenet of a healthy and happy diet.

Bengali Phal Aahar

Wash 1 cup of chivda, drain and set aside for 15 minutes. Meanwhile, peel and chop 1 cup of assorted fruits. Mix them with 1 tbsp nuts and a cup of curd. Top with some grated ginger and jaggery (optional). Dig in.

Chopped fruits, soaked chivda, and curd or milk mixed together—this dish almost sounds like desi muesli, doesn't it? But it tastes remarkably different and it's really simple to make.

Bengali Chirer Pilaf

Steam 1 cup total of green peas and diced carrots, cauliflower and beans and set it aside. Rinse 1 cup of poha under running water, fluff it up a bit and set it aside. Heat 1 tbsp oil, add 1 bay leaf, a bit of cinnamon, 2 small cardamom pods and 2 cloves. Then, add 1 sliced onion and sauté till it's translucent. Add 1 chopped boiled potato followed by the steamed vegetables, 2 sliced green chillies, 2 tbsp each of roasted peanuts and cashews, and salt, sugar and black pepper to taste. Cook for a few minutes. Toss in the rinsed poha. Cover and cook for 3–4 minutes on low heat and serve.

This dish is similar to poha but is sweeter and tastes different but absolutely delicious.

Maharashtrian Sabudana Khichdi

Wash and soak 1 cup of sabudana in water for about 2 hours. Heat 1 tbsp oil or ghee in a pan and add a pinch of mustard seeds. When they crackle, sauté ½ tsp cumin seeds, 2 sliced green chillies, a few curry leaves and a cubed boiled potato. Add 2 tbsp crushed, roasted peanuts and salt to taste. Add the soaked sabudana to this mixture. Sprinkle 1 tbsp grated fresh (or dried) coconut flakes, squeeze some lemon juice over it and eat warm.

If you remember to soak sabudana as soon as you wake up in the morning, it really takes no time to cook this delicious dish.

Panta or Pokhal

Add water to 1 cup cooked rice, cover it and leave it to ferment overnight. Next morning, add 1 sliced onion and 2 green chillies to the rice with salt and lemon and a 1 small roasted brinjal or 1 boiled, mashed potato (optional). Pair it with a home-made, tangy pickle or chutney and some curd for a perfectly healthy breakfast, teeming with probiotics that are good for your gut.

Made in the eastern part of India—mostly Orissa, Bengal and Assam—this is a fermented rice dish made from leftover rice.

Odia Soruchakli

Wash equal amounts of rice and urad dal and soak them separately overnight. Grind both separately to make a smooth paste and then mix them to make a smooth batter. To it, add salt to taste, 1 tsp each of ground or pounded fennel seeds and ginger. You can add some very finely shredded green chillies, carrots, onions, coriander leaves and mushrooms (all optional) to the mix too. Add water to the batter till it is of a spreadable consistency that is thin but not too runny. Heat and grease a non-stick pan or tawa, pour a ladle of batter and spread it evenly into a thin, round shape. Cook for a few minutes, then flip and cook on the other side. Pair it with leftover curry.

Try this pancake made with rice flour and dals as a variant to besan cheela. It is usually served with coconut or jaggery.

Tamilian Adai

Grind 1 cup of rice (soaked for 4–5 hours) and 1 cup of moong dal or any other dal you prefer (soaked for 2 hours) into a rough batter. Add a few curry leaves, ½ an inch of thinly chopped ginger, a few green chillies, 1 tomato, 1 onion, 1 tbsp sliced coconut (fresh or dry) and salt to taste. Throw in a handful of sprouts to add some crunch (optional). Then, cook it like you would cook a pancake or a dosa with some ghee and wash it down with fresh, tangy buttermilk. If you are craving sweets, pair it with powdered jaggery.

These rice and dal pancakes are my variation of the Tamilian adai. It is a really quick recipe with no fermentation required to make the batter.

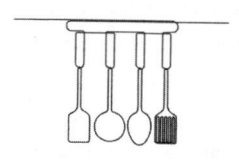

FORTY TWO

A Quick Working Lunch

For lunch, it is important that we give our body some high-quality fuel to boost our energy level and productivity at work. That is why just grabbing a cup of coffee and an aloo patty and calling that a meal does not work.

We must use the lunch hour judiciously. First, some basic rules:

- Keep your lunch light (about 500 calories or less).
- Keep it low-fat to energize you without leaving you drowsy in the afternoon.
- Make it a quick meal.

Ideally, always combine protein- and carbohydrate-rich foods. As eating just a high carbohydrate-rich meal (like a potato sandwich) raises the serotonin level in your brain, which leaves you feeling sluggish. In contrast, a meal combining protein and carbohydrates raises the norepinephrine level, which increases alertness and mental clarity and helps maintain blood sugar and energy levels throughout the day. For example, grilled fish with a slice of whole wheat bread.

LUNCH SALADS

When I say salad, if just a plate of sliced tomatoes, onions, cucumber and lettuce with a squeeze of lemon and chaat masala comes to your mind, it's time for an upgrade. Limiting a salad bowl to just these ingredients is not only boring but also a huge waste, especially when there are so many interesting ways to prepare and enjoy a salad.

Salads are a perfect mélange of all things good. Here are a few reasons why you must have salads for lunch.

- A wholesome salad is a perfect vehicle to easily bring additional nutrients, like vitamins and trace minerals, to our meals.
- It is a great way to have a plate full of antioxidants, which keep a check on free radicals, thereby reducing the chances of developing lifestyle disorders, like diabetes, heart disease, arthritis, and preventing ageing too.
- Most of us fail miserably in meeting our daily requirement of fibre, which is essential to keep our gut in good shape. A decent-sized salad a day can single-handedly address this imbalance.
- A smart salad can serve as a one-pot meal, providing the perfect mix of essential nutrients (carbohydrates, protein and good fats).
- It is, of course, a great way to cut calories from a meal without compromising on satiety.

A salad is possibly the easiest dish to put together and eat too—perfect for a working lunch. It's the best way to clean up the refrigerator and the best part is that anyone can make a salad. You don't need to spend big bucks on it or source exotic ingredients.

Putting some thought into a salad can take it from mundane to super interesting. Here are a few pointers that can help:

- A salad should have a balance of protein and carbohydrates. Greens add good carbohydrates and give the dish volume, and protein makes it more satisfying.

- Add at least one source of protein—boiled egg, tofu, cheese, lean cuts of some meat (chicken, fish, prawns) etc., to add bite and body to the salad and plump up its nutritional value too.
- Look beyond just lettuce. Instead, experiment with greens. Try the nutrient dense arugula (called 'rucola' in Italy and 'rocket' in Britain), baby spinach (you don't even need to blanch it), radicchio (to add a lovely, mildly bitter twist to the salad), watercress sprigs (it contains enough vitamin K to get you through the day) and, if you are feeling particularly adventurous, maybe even something unusual, like Japanese purple mustard.
- Challenge yourself by trying out new ingredients, like beetroots, sweet potato or avocado. Also try unusual ingredients like alfalfa and wheatgrass sprouts.
- Add a fresh fruit—like strawberry, pomegranate seeds, mango cubes or even dried fruits like prunes—to make the flavour more interesting and to get more antioxidants.
- Unusual grains—like quinoa, couscous and barley—add good carbohydrates and help add a twist to the texture too.
- Stay away from high-fat, creamy dressings and opt, instead, to make a light olive or sesame oil-based dressing with vinegar or lemon juice for some tang. It helps because the fat-soluble vitamins (A, D, E and K) need some fat to get properly absorbed in the body.
- Get a good dose of monounsaturated fats and omega-3 by adding toasted peanuts, cashews, walnuts and sunflower or sesame seeds. This also adds a nice crunch and makes the texture and taste more fun.
- Finally, sometimes add chaat masala and sometimes

sprinkle some herbs—a different one every time—to bring some extra kick to your salads.

Here are a few delicious salad recipes that are easy to put together.

Warm Bread and Vegetables Salad

Tear 1 slice of fresh bread into big chunks. Place the pieces in a large salad bowl. Add 1 sliced tomato. Season with salt, pepper and 1 tsp lime juice and set it aside for 5 minutes. Heat oil, add some garlic, followed by 1 sliced carrot and some French beans. Sauté till the vegetables are slightly tender and charred. Toss in some mushrooms and 1 sliced red pepper and cook for a few more minutes. Season with salt and pepper and add the vegetables to the salad bowl. Sprinkle some cheese and herbs of your choice and dig in!

Fruit Salad with Honey Dressing

Toss together 1 diced apple, banana and avocado each with the juice from 1 lemon, a few raisins or prunes and some mixed nuts. For the dressing, combine 1 tbsp honey, 1 tbsp orange juice, 1 tsp olive oil, ½ tsp lemon juice, 1 tsp poppy seeds, salt and mustard sauce to taste in a jar with a tight lid. Cover and shake well. Add the dressing into the salad bowl and mix thoroughly. Serve on a bed of red leaf lettuce.

Quinoa Salad

Boil ½ cup quinoa with water. Mix it with ¼ cup blanched green peas, 100 gm broccoli, 1 sliced apple and 1 sliced orange. Pour a dressing made by mixing 1 tsp vinegar, 1 tbsp olive oil and ½ tsp mustard paste into the salad. Season with salt and pepper and serve.

Spinach Salad

Blanch 200 gm spinach in hot water and squeeze it dry. To it, add ½ each of a sliced cucumber and carrot. Make a dressing with 1 tsp vinegar, 1 tbsp olive oil and ½ tsp of mustard paste and pour it in. Season with salt and pepper to taste. Finally, toss in 100 gm diced watermelon (or any seasonal fruit) and serve.

A (Reheatable) Hot Salad

Mix 200 gm steamed broccoli, 150 gm pumpkin that has been roasted in the oven at 200 °C for 30–40 minutes with a drizzle of olive oil, sprinkle of salt and pepper and 1 sliced onion. Add 100 gm of diced boiled chicken or boiled dals (or sprouts) or pan-fried tofu for added protein. Season with salt, pepper and herbs of choice and serve.

Curd and Apple Salad

In a mixing bowl, combine ¼ cup curd, ¼ cup apple juice, 1 tbsp raisin, 1 tbsp mustard sauce, 1 tsp lemon juice and ½ tsp of cinnamon powder. Toss bite-sized pieces of 2 apples in the curd mixture and refrigerate for at least 30 minutes. Arrange lettuce in a salad bowl and place the salad over it. Garnish with cherry tomatoes and thin coconut shavings.

Apple and Potato Salad

Mix 1 each of a roughly sliced carrot, apple and capsicum, ½ chopped pineapple, 100 gm sliced and blanched baby corn, and 1 roughly grated, firm boiled potato. Make a dressing by whisking together 1 tsp each of olive oil, vinegar and sugar, ½ tsp Tabasco sauce and salt, pepper and red chilli flakes to taste. Fold this dressing into the salad, chill and serve.

Beetroot Salad with Berries and Greens

Place 2 thinly sliced boiled beetroots on a plate and set them aside. In a bowl, add 3–4 torn red lettuce leaves, 100 gm sliced strawberries, salt and pepper to taste. Drizzle 1 tbsp olive oil and mix. Place this mixture on top of the thinly sliced beetroot. Garnish with 25 gm of goat cheese. Serve chilled with any healthy bread.

LUNCH BURGERS AND SANDWICHES

Salads are great, but sometimes a sandwich or burger is what you are really craving. You don't have to feel guilty because a sandwich can be made healthy too. It's all in the filling, after all. Here are a few easy, relatively healthy and comforting sandwiches and burgers that can be perfect for a work lunch.

Instant Sandwiches, 4 Ways

- Spread peanut butter on slices of whole wheat bread. Top it with sliced bananas and a few raisins and dig in.
- Spread mustard sauce on 2 slices of whole wheat bread. Place baby spinach leaves and sliced carrots between them and serve.
- Spread cream cheese on 2 slices of whole wheat bread. Place sliced ripe peaches drizzled with some honey in between and dig in.
- Whisk together hung curd with some wasabi paste and slather it on 2 slices of bread. Cut cucumber into thin slices, place it between the 2 slices and serve.

Tomato Sandwich, Spiced Up

Lightly toast 2 slices of whole wheat bread, spread a thin layer of mustard sauce on one and chilli sauce on the other. Slice tomatoes, sprinkle them with black pepper and grill or roast them in a pan till they soften. Place the tomatoes between the slices with some grated cheese and torn basil leaves sprinkled over them and dig in.

Mushrooms Toast, 3 Ways

- **Garlic mushroom toast**: In 1 tsp heated olive oil, sauté a few sliced garlic cloves for 2 minutes on low heat. Add 200 gm roughly chopped mushrooms and cook till the moisture evaporates. Season with salt, pepper, lemon juice and oregano or any other herb you have handy. Pile onto toasted whole wheat toast to dig in.
- **Grilled mushroom toast**: Sauté 1 sliced onion, 200 gm mushrooms and few garlic cloves for 5 minutes, season with salt, pepper and chilli flakes. Place the filling on a slice of bread smeared with green (coriander–mint) chutney. Top this with a slice of bread. Spread some more filling over it and sprinkle 25 gm cheese on top. Finally, add another slice smeared with green chutney. Grill or toast on a tawa on low flame till golden brown on both sides before serving.
- **Only mushrooms toast**: Sauté 100 gm sliced mushrooms in 1 tsp olive oil. Stir in salt, pepper and oregano to taste. Spread on a toast and dig in.

Chicken Eggy Delight

Make a square omelette and place it on a toast with cheese spread slathered on it. Add sliced grilled or smoked chicken (you can use leftover chicken here), tuna or salami, whatever you have handy, top it with a toast that has mustard sauce spread on it. Dig in!

Dosa Sandwich

Spread some dosa or idli batter on a greased toaster. Put any stuffing, be it leftover vegetables, boiled potato, cooked keema or scrambled eggs. This fermented sandwich turns out tastier and healthier than bread sandwich.

The Perfect Sandwich

In a bowl, mix 2 tbsp grated carrot, 1 tbsp grated cabbage, 3 tbsp hung curd, 1 mashed boiled egg, 2 lettuce leaves, a pinch of mustard powder and salt and pepper to taste. Spread the mixture evenly between two slices of toasted bread and serve.

Desi Sandwich

Instead of those greasy spreads with a hundred-odd additives, spread 2 tbsp of leftover *baingan bharta*, thick puréed dal or mashed chole on a slice of bread. Slather 1 tbsp of either sesame paste, any nut butter or mint chutney along with dried ginger powder on another slice. Add ½ each of sliced cucumber and tomatoes, 1 sliced boiled egg or sliced boiled potato between the slices. You can also add grated carrots, flame-roasted capsicums or corn kernels and enjoy!

Curd Tahini Sandwich

Make a spread using 30 gm hung curd and 20 gm tahini. Season it with salt. Take 2 slices of brown bread and spread the curd mix on them. Arrange 2 boiled egg, tomato and cucumber slices each and add 50 gm mixed lettuce on top. Finally, grill the sandwiches, season with salt and pepper to taste and serve.

Bean Spread Sandwich

Mash 1 cup of boiled rajma and mix it with 2 tbsp plain curd. Add spices and herbs—a pinch each of mustard, salt, rosemary and pepper—and a bit of olive oil. Spread this mixture over toasted rye or sourdough bread and enjoy!

Dal Burger

Soak and grind 50 gm chana dal. Add 20 gm finely chopped onion, salt, red chilli powder and amchoor to taste, 50 gm boiled potato or steamed cauliflower and mash together into a thick but rollable dough. Shape it like a patty and air-fry. Place it between 2 burger buns with some sliced cucumber and coleslaw.

Spinach-Egg Burger

In 2 tsp heated oil, cook 1 quartered tomato and 2 cloves of sliced garlic for about 4 minutes. Transfer to a bowl. In the same pan, in 1 tsp oil, sauté 1 cup spinach leaves, a pinch of red pepper flakes and ½ a chopped onion till the spinach is tender. Then, arrange the spinach back in the pan, scatter blistered tomatoes over it, season with salt and pepper. Pour 1 beaten egg over these layers, stir and scramble. Place the spinach–egg mixture between 2 burger buns and dig in.

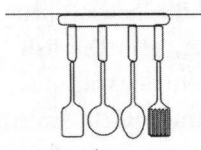

FORTY THREE

Easy, Breezy Dinners for Singles

Do you find it difficult to put together a meal when you get back home after a gruelling day at work? Here are some easy ideas that will make cooking feel like a breeze. These recipes are both healthy and easy on the pocket. Instead of ordering in, you can make these in rotation every night.

Grilled Fish with Stir-Fry Mushrooms

Grilled foods are always a good bet for people on the go. They're quick, easy to make, low-fat and nutritious. In the morning, before you leave for work, marinate 2 fillets of fish in lemon juice, salt, pepper, red chilli flakes (optional) and some crushed garlic. Just before serving, grill the fish for about 5–7 minutes on each side. Brush minimally with olive oil.

Pair the fish with this quick mushroom recipe: In 2 tsp heated olive oil, add a clove of garlic and sauté till the oil is aromatic. Add 100 gm roughly chopped mushrooms and cook for about 10 minutes, till the moisture evaporates. Season with salt, pepper, lemon juice and oregano or any other herb you prefer and serve alongside the fish.

Note: You can make this recipe with chicken too.

Spinach Salad and Sweet Potato Chaat

Wash and tear up 2 cups of spinach. Set it aside to drain. Combine cut and deseeded segments of 1 orange, a few cubes of apple, some pine nuts (*chilgoza*), the juice of 2 lemons and 2 tsp sugar. Add the spinach to this mixture. Toss well.

Pair it with this chilled sweet potato chaat: Mix 2 boiled and diced sweet potatoes with 2 tbsp crushed chivda or papad, 1 tbsp tamarind sauce, 1 tbsp curd and a few strips of cottage cheese. Make it in the morning and leave it in the refrigerator to chill all day before serving alongside the spinach salad.

Broccoli Casserole

Cut a head of broccoli into bite-sized florets and blanch until they are tender but still crunchy. Transfer into a casserole dish and add 2 tbsp cream cheese. Season with black pepper and add a bit of freshly grated cheese. Bake in a medium-hot oven until the broccoli is golden on top.

Pair it with crackers, hummus and fresh lettuce and cucumber salad simply dressed with olive oil and lemon juice.

Masor Tenga Fish with Rice

Heat 1 tbsp oil in a wok, add a pinch of mustard seeds, 1 chopped green chilli, 2 chopped tomatoes and stir till the tomatoes turn into a pulpy paste. Add some water, salt to taste and ½ tsp turmeric and boil the gravy. Slide any fried fish (preferably fried in mustard oil) into the curry and let it boil further over a low flame for a few minutes. Garnish with chopped coriander leaves and lemon juice. Serve with plain rice.

Chilled Red Rice with a Tadka

Heat 2 tbsp oil in a pan. Sauté 1 tsp mustard seeds, a few curry leaves and 1 tsp urad dal in it. Remove this tadka from pan and set it aside. In a mixing bowl, take 250 gm curd, add salt and cumin to it and mix thoroughly. Add boiled red rice to the bowl along with ½ a diced cucumber. Top it off with the prepared tadka and mix well. Refrigerate and serve cold, garnished with fried curry leaves.

Pesto Rice

Boil 1 cup of rice and set it aside. To make the pesto sauce, roughly blend a few cloves of garlic, a few basil leaves, 2 tbsp Parmesan cheese, some parsley and 8–10 walnuts (or pine nuts). Then, add 1 tbsp olive oil and blend again until a smooth sauce forms. Toss the warm, cooked rice in the pesto sauce and grate some Parmesan on top. Pair with tomato and cucumber slices and serve.

Note: Leftover pesto can be stored in a covered container in the refrigerator for upto a week or frozen for upto 3 months.

Hot Pasta

Heat 1 tbsp olive oil in a pan and sauté 1 cup chopped vegetables of your choice in it. Then, toss in sliced boiled chicken (optional). Season with salt and pepper. Mix 1 cup of boiled pasta and 1 tbsp vinegar and lemon juice each. Garnish with some fresh or dried oregano and thyme to taste. Serve hot.

Cold Pasta

Whisk together ½ cup sour cream, 1 tbsp of thousand island dressing or Caesar sauce and 1 tbsp mayonnaise till a smooth paste forms (add a little milk if needed). Toss in 1 cup of boiled pasta, a few salami slices and salt, pepper and herbs to taste. Serve chilled.

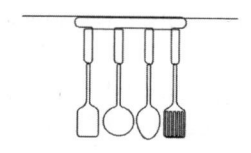

FORTY FOUR

One-Bowl Meals

Bowls are the new plates. All sorts of interesting meals are now being eaten in a bowl, ranging from protein bowls, Buddha bowls, broth bowls, quinoa bowls and globowls (globally inspired bowl meals). Similarly, breakfast bowls, including smoothie bowls, acai bowls and Banzai bowls are all the rage. You only have to Google them and you'll be bowled over.

THE BENEFITS OF ONE-BOWL MEALS

One-bowl meals are a great addition to your meals, here's why:

- You can create your own one-bowl dish based on your preferences and health restrictions. The best part is that it is good for all meals from breakfast to dinner. In the morning, you can have a balanced, quick and easy breakfast with a bowl that includes fruit, curd and whole grains.
- They are a great way to blend multiple flavours and fit in a huge variety of ingredients—even the ones that you don't usually eat, like sprouts or chickpeas—in a single dish.
- A bowl is a great way of getting your proteins, carbohydrates, fibre and nutrients (vitamins and minerals) in the right proportion.

- They are a great way to eat your vegetables—most bowl recipes demand a good quantity of vegetables, so you get a fibre and antioxidant boost.
- They are a great way to combine different vegetables with different kinds of whole grains—like quinoa, farro, amaranth, pearl barley, brown rice or soba—and protein sources, like grilled meats, eggs, beans, nuts, cheese or tofu.
- If you want to go grain-free, you can just opt for zucchini noodles or cauliflower rice and you are set. In a bowl, you won't miss the roti and rice as much.
- They get the gastric juices moving, easing digestion and keeping our guts happy.
- They help reduce the need to put together time-consuming dishes to make a meal seem complete. So, they save time as well.
- Finally, eating from a bowl is a good way to monitor your portion size and thus calorie intake. This gladdens my nutritionist heart immensely because it can be a big help to those struggling with weight issues. They leave you feeling satisfied and great, and let you stay comfortably full till the next meal, which also reduces snacking between meals.

BREAKFAST

A Bowl with an Asian twist

Top 1 cup of cooked amaranth grain with 1 cup of chopped, stir-fried or steamed vegetables of your choice and ½ cup pan-fried tofu. Top it with a drizzle of a silky tahini sauce and serve.

To make the tahini sauce, add ½ cup tahini (sesame seeds paste), ¼ cup lemon juice, ¼ tsp sea salt and ¼ tsp garlic powder or 1 minced garlic clove to a small mixing bowl and whisk to combine. Add a little water at a time (about 6 tbsp) and continue whisking until you have a creamy, pourable sauce.

LUNCH

One-Pot Quick Meal

Sauté 1 cup of vegetables (frozen peas, corn kernels or baby corn, spinach leaves, mushrooms, mixed frozen veggies, etc.) with a bit of tomato, some herbs and strips of ginger and garlic and salt to taste. Then, add 1 cup of rice and 2.5 cups of water and cook till it is almost done. Mix in a beaten egg to cook at the last minute or add some boiled, shredded chicken for a completely nutritious one-bowl meal.

Quick Vegetable Bowl

Steam 1 cup of vegetables (beans, carrots, baby corn, pepper, onions) in water for 10 minutes. In a pan, heat 1 tbsp of olive oil, add the vegetables and sauté for 5 minutes. Season with salt, pepper, dried oregano and fresh basil. Transfer to a plate, top off with 50 gm paneer strips and serve.

DINNER

Beetroot Greens Pesto Bowl

In a food processor, combine 4 cups of beetroot greens (with their stems removed), 4 crushed cloves of garlic, ½ cup walnuts, 3 tbsp grated Parmesan, ½ tsp salt and ¼ tsp black pepper. Blend the ingredients while pouring up to ½ cup extra virgin olive oil to it until the mixture reaches the consistency of pesto sauce. Store the sauce in an airtight container in the fridge. Take 2 tbsp of the pesto and toss in assorted steamed vegetables, some chopped cashews and half an apple. Add a few slices of avocado for good fats and serve.

Coconut Rice with Green Lentils

Combine 1 cup of rice, 3 cups of coconut water, 1 cup of light coconut milk and salt to taste and bring to a boil. Reduce the heat to a simmer, cover and cook for 5 minutes. Stir in ½ cup of boiled green lentils. Cover and cook till the rice is done. Dig in!

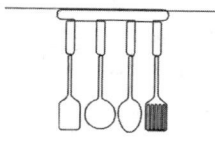

FORTY FIVE

Leftover Delights

The Covid lockdown taught many of us to make the most of the resources that we have at hand. This realization came about because, for the first time in recent history, we all faced a situation where sourcing simple everyday groceries that are usually easily accessible, like a loaf of bread or some fresh vegetables, often became a challenge. So, we all started making do with what we had and learnt to prudently reuse leftovers (something our grandparents always did by default). The big lesson here is that it makes sense to not waste anything, and when it comes to food, we can and must eat it all.

CHANGE HOW YOU UTILIZE LEFTOVERS

Here are some simple recipes made from leftovers that get ready in a jiffy.

Phodni Chi Poli

Roughly grind leftover rotis for a few seconds and set aside. Make a tadka with mustard seeds, hing, cumin seeds and some finely sliced onion and green chillies and add the ground rotis to it. Season with salt and some sugar. Let it cook for a minute before serving. Pair it with buttermilk or raita and a fruit chaat for a delicious, satisfying meal.

When you just don't have anything handy, you can still make

this Maharashtrian dish made from leftover rotis.

Leftover Aloo Chaat

Mix 2 tbsp crushed chivda or roasted papad, 1 tbsp of tamarind sauce, 1 tbsp curd, a handful of raw or slightly steamed sprouts of your choice or boiled kala chana or green moong dal (if you have it handy) and a few slices of cucumber to leftover jeera aloo or any other potato preparation. Top it with a few strips of paneer or just crush some cheese. Chill for 30 minutes before digging in.

Egg-Roti Mix

Place a poached egg on a leftover roti. Top it with tomato salsa (or ketchup), chopped chillies, fresh coriander leaves, some grated carrot, beetroot and steamed spinach (or any vegetables you have handy). Roll it up and enjoy!

Spinach Delight

Do you have leftover spinach sabzi or stir-fry from last night? Heat 1 tbsp olive oil, add the leftover spinach, a pinch of grated nutmeg and salt and pepper to taste. Garnish with 50 gm feta or any other cheese you have. Pair it with a big serving of simple kachumbar salad with tomato, onion and cucumber and dig in.

Leftover Dal Tikki

Dry out leftover dal in a pan over low heat. Mix it thoroughly with a finely chopped onion, salt and spices, like red chilli powder, cumin seeds etc., to taste, and a boiled, mashed potato or some steamed cauliflower. Shape the mixture into patties and air-fry or pan-fry. Place the patties between burger buns with sliced cucumber and onions in the middle or just pair them with a nice salad on the side and dig in!

Cheesy Vegetables

Reheat any leftover vegetables you may have in a pan with lots of garlic, a mashed potato and a bit of cheese. Enjoy!

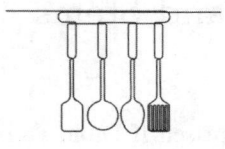

FORTY SIX

Reusing Peels and Stems

Would you be surprised if I told you that I am a big peel eater, and that I often prefer them over actual food? Often, while peeling peas, I chew the soft centre of the peels along with raw peas?

Ample research shows that discarding peels is like throwing away the best, healthiest part of our produce because they have the maximum concentration of vitamins, minerals and antioxidants. They are also low-calorie and virtually free of fat, cholesterol and sugar. Perhaps chewing on the peels of peas might be going a little too far, but, trust me, it pays off big time to keep the peels on while eating most fruits and vegetables.

༄

STORY TIME

It seems that many Indian households have always known the importance of peels. 'Bengalis have a long history of cooking with vegetable peels. It's frugal, sustainable and, most importantly, delicious,' said **Madhumita Pyne**, a Mumbai-based film-maker turned home chef and caterer. 'One of my favourites is *lau-er khosha bhaja*. As a child, I use to absolutely loathe *lau* or bottle gourd. But I would still be super excited whenever it was cooked at home because it would also mean I would get to eat the peels! The peels are julienned and stir-fried in mustard oil with salt-turmeric and a little sprinkling of poppy seeds. Super simple but so delectable! We would also cook potato skins similarly,' she shared.

CHANGE HOW YOU COOK WITH PEELS AND STEMS

Here are a few simple, delicious and super healthy recipes that utilize peels and stems.

Note: If you are worried about pesticides and other contaminants on peels and stems, wash fruits and vegetables thoroughly with water first. Then, wash them with 1 part vinegar mixed with 4 parts water. Wash them again with cold water and then gently pat them dry using a soft cloth.

Aloo Bhujia with Bitter Gourd Peels

Peel 500 gm bitter gourd, sprinkle some salt on it and set it aside for 30 minutes. Then, wash it with water and squeeze it dry. In a pan, heat 1 tsp mustard oil and crackle some mustard seeds in it. Sauté 1 thinly sliced medium-sized onion in it till it's pink. Then, toss in 1 chopped boiled potato and season the mixture with salt, red chilli powder and amchoor powder. Stir-fry for 3 minutes. Finally, add the grated bitter gourd skin and cook it till it's done. Sprinkle some amchoor powder on top before serving.

Sprouts Sabzi with Bottle Gourd Peels

Wash and chop the peels of a bottle gourd and set them aside. Stir-fry 1 sliced onion and 1 small cubed potato. Season with salt and red chilli powder to taste. Toss in the chopped peels along with 2 tbsp of any sprouts. Sprinkle some water over the dish, cover and cook till it's done. Pair with roti.

Danthal Khatta Meetha

In 1 tbsp heated oil, crackle ½ tsp cumin seeds and sauté 1 chopped onion till it's golden. Add ½ tbsp ginger garlic paste and cook for a few minutes. Season with ½ tsp red chilli powder, 1 tsp coriander powder, ½ tsp turmeric and ½ tsp pav bhaji masala and sauté for a minute. Add the purée of 2 tomatoes. Cook till the oil separates. Toss in 250 gm cauliflower stalks and some cauliflower leaves along with some salt to taste. Pour in ½ cup water and pressure cook for 1 whistle. Once cooked, add garam masala, garnish with coriander leaves and serve.

Mixed Peels Stir-Fry

In some heated mustard oil, add a pinch of kalonji, 1 green chilli, ½ chopped onion, 1 chopped potato and 1 cup of any chopped peels—potato, pumpkin or bottle gourd—you may have handy. Season with salt to taste and a pinch of turmeric and cook till the peels are done.

Tangy Lemony Herbal Oil

To 1 cup olive oil, add 1 tbsp grated lemon peel, a generous bunch of fresh thyme or basil, 1 tsp each of chilli flakes and granulated garlic and a few whole black peppercorns. Let it infuse before using. It's the perfect dressing for salads or marinade for meats.

Potato Peel Crisps

Wash and dry potato peels. Sprinkle some besan, salt, turmeric and red chilli powder over them and set them aside. Temper mustard seeds in some heated oil and stir-fry the coated peels in it till they are crisp.

For a baked version, just wash and thoroughly dry the peels. Toss them in a little oil and season them with salt and red chilli flakes or any herbs of your choice. Bake them in a preheated oven for 12–15 minutes at 180 °C.

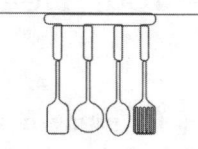

FORTY SEVEN

Meals to Make Your Heart Happy

Some good diet rules for eating heart-healthy are eating a low-sodium, low-fat diet that is high in antioxidants and heart-healthy nutrients. A smart strategy to keep your heart healthy is to control the risk factors—like blood pressure, cholesterol, homocysteine and inflammation—by eating specific risk-mitigating foods. Here are a few delicious and easy meals to make your heart happy.

Granola

Mix 2 cups of rolled oats with 1 cup of dried fruits, seeds and a little brown sugar. Toast for 3–5 minutes in an oven preheated to 200 °C, stirring a couple of times to avoid burning. Cool before storing in an airtight container.

Note: High cholesterol is a big risk factor for heart disease. Oats are an effective cholesterol-buster, as their soluble fibre reduces the absorption of cholesterol in the bloodstream and helps throw it out of our system.

Almond Butter

Roast a few almonds for 10 minutes in a preheated oven at 200 °C, stirring halfway. Let them cool for about 10 minutes. While they're warm, grind them until they are creamy in a high-speed blender, adding small batches at a time. Keep scraping down the sides as necessary. Add a pinch of cinnamon and a tsp of olive oil while blending to make the butter creamier.

Note: All cholesterol is not bad. In fact, high-density lipoprotein (HDL) cholesterol removes bad cholesterol from the arteries and prevents fatty plaque build-up in them. Almonds are a perfect to help raise our HDL levels because they are loaded with good fat (monounsaturated fatty acid), vitamin E, magnesium and folic acid, which are all good for our heart.

Salmon Sandwich

Combine 100 gm chopped, boneless and cooked salmon, 1 cucumber, a few tbsp curd and 1 tbsp of lemon juice in a small bowl. Spread a thin layer of butter on the cut sides of sandwich buns and top them with lettuce. Spoon the salmon mixture between the buns. Chill before serving.

Note: Salmon is brilliant for our heart health because it delivers protein and helps keeps inflammation in check, which is a big risk factor for heart disease.

Garlic Dip, 2 Ways

- Combine 3 cloves of crushed garlic, 3 tbsp sour cream, 1 tbsp ketchup, salt and pepper to taste and mix well.
- Whisk 200 gm hung curd, 1 tsp finely chopped garlic, 2 tsp chopped coriander leaves, 1 small chopped onion, a few drops of red chilli sauce and salt and crushed pepper to taste until a smooth dip forms.

Note: Garlic contains sulphide compounds that not only reduce cholesterol but also prevent and remove clots, which are a big risk factor for heart attacks.

Orange Smoothie

Blend together 1 peeled orange, 1 cup of low-fat yoghurt or milk, ice cubes and a splash of vanilla until the mixture reaches the consistency of a smoothie. Serve chilled.

Note: The antioxidant vitamin C in oranges protects the artery walls. The folic acid in oranges aids the disposal of artery-clogging homocysteine from our bodies.

Spinach Feta Delight

Wilt spinach in olive oil over a medium heat for a few minutes. Then, stir in a pinch of grated nutmeg and feta cheese and dig in.

Note: Spinach is high in folate, which keeps the levels of homocysteine low. High homocysteine damages the blood vessels and increases blood clotting.

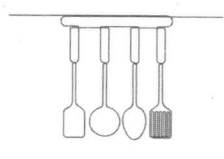

FORTY EIGHT

Healthy Rainy-Day Recipes

Who doesn't like the rains? After all, everything gets green and beautiful all around us because of them. However, the onset of monsoons can be dicey for our health, and it is better to be safe than sorry during this season.

Rains bring a lot of challenges, including increased appetite. There can be many reasons for this. When the sky is overcast or sunlight is blocked due to the rains, serotonin production goes down, which increases carbohydrate cravings and makes you hungry. Additionally, as the temperature drops, our bodies burn more energy to stay warm, which, in turn, increases our appetites. So, it is very important to eat right during this season for the following reasons:

- Our digestion is compromised due to high humidity. So, it is important to stick to easily digestible foods.
- Constipation and water retention are common during the monsoon. Furthermore, infections are at an all-time high because our immunity tends to be compromised during this season.

CHANGE WHAT YOU COOK DURING THE MONSOON

Monsoon meals are a little tricky and what we put on our plates has to be well thought out. Here are a few foods to include in your diet based on the issues you may face during monsoon.

Raw Banana for Constant Hunger

Raw bananas are very high in RS. The short-chain fatty acids produced by the fermentation of RS in the intestines not only keeps one full for longer but also increases the ability of the body to absorb nutrients, especially calcium. Here is a quick and easy raw banana recipe.

Raw Banana Thoran

Boil 1 cubed raw banana in water with turmeric powder and salt. Remove from water when the pieces are soft and set aside.

In heated oil, temper mustard seeds, 2–3 cloves of crushed garlic, 1 small chopped onion, 2 dried red chillies and a few curry leaves. Sauté till light brown in colour. Toss in the cooked banana cubes and serve hot.

Bitter Gourd to Combat Constipation

Bitter gourd has a lot going for it. It is a known immunity booster that protects us against the seasonal flu. Its blood-purifying properties help keep infections at bay. It's also a good digestive, as it stimulates the secretion of gastric juices that aid digestion and keep constipation at bay.

Spiced Bitter Gourd

Vertically slit 5–6 small bitter gourds, leaving their stems intact. Sprinkle salt, red chilli powder and pepper to taste over the bitter gourds, thoroughly rubbing them into the slits. Tie up each bitter gourd with a clean thread to secure the spices inside it. Reserve the remaining spices.

Peel and chop 2 onions and stir-fry them in a little oil till they start to change colour. Remove them from the oil and let them sit on a kitchen towel to drain the excess oil. Add the spiced bitter gourds to the pan and fry on medium–low heat till they start to brown. Sprinkle half of the leftover masala onto them and stir-fry for another 3–4 minutes. Sprinkle the remaining masala on the onions or smear it into the slits in the bitter gourds. Mix the bitter gourds and onions together and serve.

Corn to Solve Sluggish Digestion

There is a reason why corn is in season during the monsoons—it delivers a lot of fibre, which keeps our digestion on track. Even when our digestion gets a little sluggish during the rains, corn does so much good for our gut, thanks to its high ratio of insoluble to soluble fibre. Here's a quick corn recipe.

Quick Corn

Toss 200 gm of steamed corn kernels in an olive oil, salt, pepper and herbs of your choice to taste and enjoy!

Sprouts to Stop Feeling Fatigued

Sprouts help generate enzymes that the body needs to function properly, stay at its efficient best and keep lethargy away. They also make immunity-boosting nutrients more bioavailable.

Quick Sprouts Salad

Take 1 cup of sprouts (I like them raw; you can steam them if you wish), 5–6 cherry tomatoes, and a hard-boiled egg; combine and sprinkle salt and pepper on top.

Banana to Avoid Bloating

Banana is the perfect fruit to reduce bloating, as it is loaded with potassium. It also has a high iron content, so it can stimulate haemoglobin production in the bloodstream and help keep monsoon-induced fatigue away.

Meetha Banana Poha

In a small bowl, add 1 chopped banana, 2 tbsp jaggery paste, 1 tbsp grated coconut (fresh or dried) and a pinch of cardamom powder. Add the mixture to ½ a cup of soaked and rinsed poha. Then, stir in ½ cup of warm milk into the mixture. Garnish with some raisins and chopped cashews and dig in.

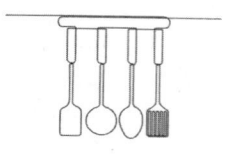

FORTY NINE

Chutney Love

One ground rule of eating better for your health is to ensure that we have enough micronutrients (vitamins and minerals) in our diet on a daily basis. These micronutrients, known as such because they are needed in very small quantities, are extremely potent and can help keep our health, weight and body functioning on track. The easiest way to fill the nutritional gaps in our diet is by eating a dollop of a home-made chutney every day, at least with one meal.

∽

STORY TIME

Subha J. Rao, a Mangalore-based journalist and founder of a range of home-roasted, home-ground artisanal spice mixes, Made in Mangalore By Subha (madeinmangalore.in), confirmed that for a South Indian person, chutney is a part and parcel of culinary tradition. 'And no, coconut or white chutney, coriander or green chutney and tomato or red chutney are not the only chutneys we make. And we don't eat chutney only with idli, dosa, *paniyaaram* or *uthappam*. We eat a whole lot of them, made with vegetables, peels and rice too,' she said.

A favourite in her home is *kempu* (red) chutney. The

combination of coarsely ground and roasted toor and chana dals, chillies, hing, tamarind and grated coconut is a winner and is usually eaten with *ganji*, which is red or brown rice cooked to a semi-mush and served with grated coconut, salt and some golden, melting ghee. 'It's what lifts everyone's weary souls when there's a fever going around or when one feels peckish but is not in any great mood to cook,' she said.

Another favourite from her childhood is ridge gourd peel chutney, which uses the same ingredients as kempu, along with gently sautéed and crushed ridge gourd peel.

She also absolutely loves the incredibly cooling Karnataka *thambli*. This chutney is made by whisking curd with some local spices and herbs, ajwain leaves, tender guava leaves, coriander and curry leaves, garnished with some coconut.

Subha J. Rao's Brinjal Chutneys, 2 Ways

- **Roasted brinjal chutney:** Roast 1 brinjal over a direct flame, à la baingan bharta. Sauté $1/2$ each of a chopped onion and tomato, 1 inch grated ginger, 2 chopped green chillies with a pinch of hing and turmeric, and add the roasted brinjal to the mix. Garnish with coriander leaves. The dish is quite like baingan bharta, but without garam masala.
- **Kathirikkai bajji:** Chop 1 onion, 1 tomato, a bit of garlic, ginger and a few green chillies. Sauté them in a bit of oil and then add 1 chopped potato and 2 chopped small- or medium-sized brinjals and salt to taste. Cook till the potato is soft and mash it all together. Drizzle some fresh coconut oil and garnish with coriander leaves.

CHANGE THE WAY YOU COOK CHUTNEYS

Here are a few delicious chutney recipes that are easy to make.

Raw Mango Chutney

Chop 250 gm raw mangoes and grind them to a coarse paste with 2 red chillies, a pinch of hing, 2 tbsp desiccated coconut, 2 tbsp jaggery and salt to taste. Temper some curry leaves in 1 tsp heated mustard oil and pour this tadka over the prepared chutney before serving.

Tamarind Chutney

Boil 100 gm tamarind in water. Deseed it and grind the cooked flesh into a paste. To it, add 50 gm jaggery, a pinch of dried ginger powder and black salt and black pepper to taste. Cook this mixture down for a few minutes, mashing it until it is smooth and serve.

Amla Chutney, 2 Ways

- **Meethi chutney:** Deseed 500 gm amla, cover and boil till they are soft. Transfer these to a pot with 300 ml water, 300 gm sugar and 1 star anise. Boil this on very low heat while stirring constantly till the water reduces and a thick paste forms. Cool and blend the reduced mixture with a pinch of black salt. Cool it and store in an airtight glass bottle.
- **Sugar-free amla chutney:** Boil 2 deseeded amlas till they are soft and mash them. Grind ½ a cucumber and 2 green chillies. Mix everything together with 1 tsp hot mustard oil and add salt to taste before serving.

Coriander Chutney, 2 Ways

- **Coriander leaf chutney:** Grind 100 gm coriander leaves and 2 cloves of garlic. Add an inch of ginger, 2 green chillies

and grind again with a little water. Finish it off with some lemon juice and serve.
- **Coriander stem chutney:** Fry a green chilli in a little bit of oil for a minute. Hand pound the fried chilli, 100 gm coriander stems, 2 cloves of garlic and a few roasted peanuts together. Add salt to taste and squeeze in some lemon juice before serving.

Peanut Chutney

Grind 50 gm peanuts, 1 tomato, an inch of ginger and 2 green chillies together. Add salt to taste. Make a tadka in mustard oil with some mustard seeds and curry leaves. Pour it over the chutney and serve.

Onion Chutney

Heat a little bit of oil and add mustard and methi seeds and curry leaves to it. Fry 3 tsp of urad dal, 2 chopped onions, 5 red chillies, 2–3 cashews and an inch of tamarind to the oil. Let it cool. Grind everything to a smooth paste and enjoy!

Watermelon Rind Chutney

Separate the pink inner flesh and trim off the outer green skin of a watermelon from its rind. Dice the rind into ½ inch pieces. In a pan, add 3 cups of the cubed rind, ½ cup sugar, ½ cup minced ginger, 1 tbsp each of chopped green chillies and garlic, ½ cup vinegar, ½ cup water, 2–3 crushed black peppercorns and ½ tsp salt. Bring it to a boil over medium heat, then let it simmer for 50 minutes. Keep stirring till all the sugar dissolves and the rind becomes translucent and tender. Let the mixture cool, transfer into an airtight container and chill for a day to let the flavours settle before serving.

Garlic Chutney

Sauté 30 gm garlic and 2 green chillies in mustard oil for a few minutes. Take it off the heat and it is ready to eat.

Tomato Onion Chutney

Heat a little oil, add 3 chopped tomatoes, 1 chopped onion, 2 chopped green chillies and a few cloves of garlic. Cook for 5–7 minutes and serve.

Ash Gourd Peel Chutney

Peel an ash gourd. Finely chop the peels and boil them in a little water till they are soft. Grind them with a little coconut, fried green chillies, lemon juice and ginger. Dig in!

A Quick Mango Chutney

In ½ tsp oil, lightly fry 2 pulped mangoes, ½ tsp red chilli flakes, ½ tsp methi seeds and salt to taste. Your chutney is ready.

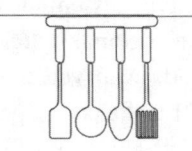

FIFTY

In a Pickle!

Our traditional thali always has a dollop of pickle, and there is a huge variety of them to pick from. No meal is considered complete without pickles. Now, science tells us that our ancestors have been health smart, and we are actually reaping the benefits of pickles, some of which have been listed below.

- They are full of good bacteria, called probiotics, which are great for our gut health.
- They are loaded with multiple antioxidants, which are potent disease fighters.
- They are low-calorie but have high nutrient density. Pickles deliver many essential vitamins and minerals and help fill in nutritional deficiencies.
- Pickles make food, even vegetables that we don't quite like, palatable. This helps us gain the benefits of the foods we would otherwise not have eaten.
- Finally, good pickles are comfort foods. They almost always have some good memories attached to them, which can help cheer people up.

Some things to keep in mind while having pickles.

- The best kind of pickles are home-made, as the traditional way of making them, through fermentation, makes them naturally probiotic. Thus, when eaten moderately (a small piece with every meal), they not only help improve digestion but also increase the good bacteria in our gut, which boost our immunity and improve the absorption of nutrients from the food we eat. With home-made pickles, one can control both the quality and quantity of ingredients, avoid poor-quality vegetables, oil and spices while keeping the salt, sugar and oil content as low as desired.

- With pickles, less is more. So, make sure you eat them like a pickle and not like a sabzi. The way your nani used to.
- The biggest health problem with ready-made pickles available in the market is that they tend to have high oil and salt content, which can be detrimental to both our heart and blood pressure in the long run.
- If you are watching your weight, it is best to stick to pickles made in brine rather than oil-based pickles, as oil can add extra calories to your diet. Furthermore, if the quality of the oil is suspect, it may even add trans fats to your diet.
- If you have blood pressure issues, go easy on brined pickles as well or rinse them before eating because a single serving of an average pickle can deliver 500–1,100 mg sodium—that's almost half of the recommended sodium allowance for an entire day! The high salt content may also cause bloating and water retention and even reduce calcium absorption, which can lead to low bone density.
- Diabetics must avoid sweet pickles or exercise portion control while eating them.

I believe that with the health benefits they offer, giving up pickles because you are scared of their oil or salt content is not a good idea. One should, instead, eat them in moderation. The solution may be as simple as making your own pickles at home and eating them in small portions at a time.

With this in mind, here are a few delicious pickle recipes that are also easy to make.

Andhra Cucumber Pickle

In a wide vessel, mix together 2 cups of deseeded and finely chopped cucumbers, 3 tbsp red chilli powder, 3 tbsp mustard powder and 1.5 tbsp salt. Slowly incorporate 4 tbsp sesame oil and combine till all the pieces are well-coated. Store in a covered jar and keep it in a dark, moisture-free place overnight. It will be ready to eat the next day.

Bitter Gourd Pickle

Chop 250 gm bitter gourd into thin, long pieces. In 1 tbsp heated oil, temper a pinch of mustard seeds, 1 inch sliced ginger, 2–3 cloves of crushed garlic, 2 chopped green chillies and a few curry leaves. Add the bitter gourd to this mixture and sauté well. Sprinkle turmeric, chilli and methi powders and hing to taste. Pour 100 ml vinegar and cook for a few minutes. Season with salt to taste and 1 tsp sugar. Let it cool before storing in a container.

Rajasthani Aam Achaar

To 500 gm peeled and chopped raw mango, add 100 gm salt, ½ tsp of hing and about ½ tsp chilli powder to taste. Mix well and store in an airtight bottle for 3 days before digging in.

Lemon Rind Pickle

Chop the rinds of 10 lemons, sprinkle them with 1–2 tsp salt and refrigerate for 2 days. Then, add 2 tsp chilli powder, some turmeric and mix well. In 1 tbsp heated oil, add a pinch of mustard seeds, a few curry leaves, a pinch of hing, some sliced garlic and ginger and the prepared lemon rinds. Squeeze the juice of 2 lemons and about 30 gm jaggery into the mixture and stir till everything is well-coated. Switch off the gas, cool and store in a bottle.

Khajoor Achaar

Clean, wash and remove the seeds from 250 gm dates and cut them into thin pieces. Make a syrup with 50 gm sugar and water. In a pan, with heated oil, crackle mustard seeds, sliced ginger and curry leaves. Then, add hing and turmeric, red chilli and methi powders to taste. To this, add the dates, pour in the sugar syrup and 25 gm honey. Cook for a few minutes. Cool and refrigerate.

Amla Achaar

Steam 10 amlas for 10 minutes and then deseed them, separating them into segments. Let them cool. Heat 1 tbsp oil, add a pinch each of mustard seeds and hing. Take the pan off the heat and stir in the segmented, steamed amlas into the tadka. Then, add red chilli powder, turmeric and salt to taste and mix well. Finally, sprinkle pickle masala (dry roast mustard, methi and fennel seeds till they turn golden, then blend them to a fine powder) on top, give it one final mix and store.

Meetha Nimbu Adrak Achaar

To 250 gm chopped lemons, add ½ cup of salt, 2 cups of sugar, ½ cup chilli powder and 50 gm sliced ginger. Mix well. Store in a dry glass jar and keep it in the sun for a week before digging in.

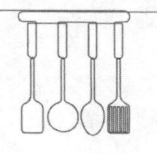

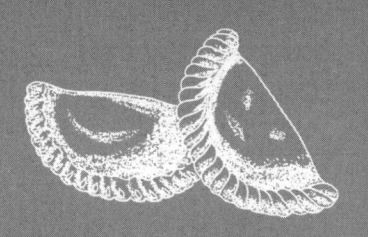

Part 9

Guilt-Free Festival Feasting

I take a slightly different approach to festival snacking. I believe that during festive months, we must closely monitor our diet and consciously control it to undo the damage that excessive snacking and consumption of sweets might cause.

I believe that the damage caused by festive foods can be undone (and even prevented) by consciously adopting time-tested nutritional rules. These include intentionally incorporating some healthy, cleansing and strengthening foods in our diet, even during festivals, and enjoying these happy times with as much home-cooked food as possible.

For truly guilt-free festival feasting, this section covers healthy but delicious sweets, snacks and even festive gifts.

FIFTY ONE

The Delicious Grains of Navratri

There's lots going for Navratri fasts and I am all for them. Fasting helps rest and unburden the body. It lets our bodies refresh and recover from within while cleansing them—a natural detox, if you please!

The food eaten during a fast is very logically designed to not just give our body and taste buds a break from our regular fare but also rotate our grains and go gluten-free for the changing season, thereby detoxing and cleansing the body from within. Surely you have noticed that both the Navratris fall during a season change—from winter to summer and again when the air begins to get nippy and our immunity is low.

Here are a few delicious recipes made with the 5 main grains eaten during Navratri to make the fasting season both healthy and tasty for you.

Kuttu or Buckwheat Flour

Buckwheat flour is packed with high-quality protein. It also contains the amino acid lysine, which is missing from most of our staple grains, like wheat and rice. This a big plus, especially for vegetarians. It is loaded with fibre as well, which helps keep hunger pangs and cravings at bay.

To change the way you cook buckwheat this festive season, skip kuttu pakora and try buckwheat noodles instead.

Buckwheat Noodles for Fasting

Boil 50 gm buckwheat noodles in water. Add some stir-fried vegetables (that your fast allows). Season with spices allowed during your fast according to taste. Squeeze some lemon juice on top, garnish with nuts and dig in. This tastes nice chilled as well.

Sabudana

Sabudana is a good source of carbohydrates that delivers the much-needed energy boost when we are fasting. It is also easy to digest.

If you bored of the same old sabudana khichdi, try sabudana kheer instead.

Sabudana Kheer

Wash and soak ½ cup of sabudana in about ½ cup of water for 2–3 hours, till it becomes light and fluffy. Boil 2 cups of milk on sim for about 10 minutes, stirring constantly. Then, add the sabudana to the milk and cook for about 5 minutes till it becomes translucent. Sprinkle 2 tbsp sugar, a pinch of cardamom powder, some chopped pistachios and a few strands of saffron (optional) into the boiling mixture. Boil for another 2 minutes. Let the kheer thicken as it cools. Chill and eat after some time.

Amaranth Flour

This underrated grain is a fantastic source of protein that you must try out this fasting season and continue eating even after.

If you find amaranth rotis boring, try an amaranth pancake instead.

Amaranth Pancake

Thoroughly mix 30 gm amaranth flour, 200 ml milk, 30 gm desiccated coconut, a pinch of salt, baking powder and water (if needed). Season with 1 tbsp honey and a pinch of cinnamon powder. Heat a non-stick frying pan, smear some oil on it and pour a dollop of the amaranth batter evenly into a round pancake. Cook on both sides on low heat. Drizzle some honey on top and serve.

Samak Rice

Samak rice (barnyard millet) is a millet that is easy to digest and gluten-free. It has higher protein content than regular rice. This festive season, skip the regular samak rice pilaf and try it in the form of a dhokla instead.

Samak Rice Dhokla

Soak 1 cup of samak rice and ½ cup of sabudana in water for 3 hours. Drain it and grind well. Stir in about ½ cup of sour curd in the ground batter. Leave it to ferment overnight. Before making the dhokla, add 1 tsp Eno to the batter and fasting salt to taste. Steam the batter in a steamer or pressure cooker without the whistle for about 30 minutes to make dhoklas.

Singhara or Water Chestnut Flour

Singhara flour is made by peeling, drying and grinding singhara. It is not just gluten-free but low-calorie too. Instead of having the same old singhara roti and pakoras, try singhara halwa.

Singhara Halwa

Roast ½ cup of singhara flour in ghee for about 5–7 minutes till it turns light brown. Then, add 1 cup of boiled, extremely hot water to the flour, stirring continuously to avoid lumps. In about 2–3 minutes, when the water is completely absorbed, add ⅓ cup of sugar and stir again till the ghee starts to separate from the halwa. Take it off the flame, sprinkle a pinch of cardamom powder and some chopped almonds on top and serve warm.

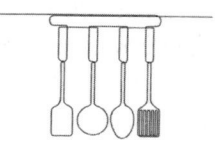

FIFTY TWO

Diwali Ready with Healthy Snacks

What's Diwali without sumptuous dinners, lots of sweets and unlimited snacking? Food is definitely a big part of this festival. But who says you have to eat or feed others unhealthy snacks when they come to wish you on Diwali? It's time to shift towards healthier Diwali snacks. Here are a few simple, super healthy sweet as well as savoury snacks for Diwali.

Chocolate Peanut Butter Flaxseed Granola

Mix 150 gm chocolate chips, 60 gm peanut butter, 2 tbsp roasted flaxseeds, 2 tbsp honey, 250 gm oats until the mixture starts clumping together. Spread it evenly on a greased baking sheet and bake for 10 minutes at 200 °C. When it cools, cut into bite-sized pieces and keep them handy for guests.

Note: With this snack, you deliver multiple antioxidants and minerals from chocolate, energy from the complex carbohydrates in oats and good fat from peanut butter and flaxseeds.

Chia Seed Pudding with Nuts

Mix 1 tbsp chia seeds in 100 ml milk (or almond milk) along with some assorted nuts and 1 tbsp honey. Stir well. Chill in the fridge for 3 hours to thicken. Transfer the mixture into cups depending as many servings as you need.

Note: This snack provides fibre and protein from chia seeds along with multiple other micronutrients and calcium from milk. It is also a high-satiety snack.

Hummus on Toast

Soak chickpeas overnight. Next morning, boil them till they are soft. Cool and then blend them with garlic, tahini paste and olive oil. Drizzle some olive oil on a whole wheat toast, spread the hummus on top, cut the toast into squares and serve.

Note: This delicious snack has a good combination of proteins and carbohydrates.

Low-Calorie Pakoras

Make a pakora mix by adding besan to cut onions and boiled potatoes. Coat a non-stick pan with 1 tsp oil. Arrange dollops of the pakora mix in the pan and cover it. In just a couple of minutes, the pakora will puff up. Flip them to cook the other side and serve hot.

Note: Not only do these pakoras cook fast and taste divine, they are also loaded with the protein-rich goodness of besan!

Cheese and Fruits Skewer

Cut grapes, apples, pineapples and cheddar cheese into small, equal-sized cubes. Skewer the cheese and the fruits alternately. Chill and serve.

Note: These skewers are a favourite among fruit lovers and manage to convert those who aren't too fond of fruits into fruit eaters. The cheese delivers calcium and protein while fruits bring loads of fibre and satiety.

FIFTY THREE

Gifting Some Home-Made Happiness

Growing up, I remember how much I used to look forward to the platefuls of home-made delicacies (covered nicely with a lacy, embroidered cloth) arriving from family friends' houses during Diwali. We would get to eat *manda pitha* from Orissa, *puran poli* or *narali bhaat* from Maharashtra, *mishti doi* or *rosogullas* from West Bengal and so on. And my mum would send back kheer or suji halwa laden with dry fruits that everyone loved. I still remember those days, that taste and the anticipation that kept us children happy and excited throughout the festive season.

Now, of course, packed dabbas from the halwais arrive as Diwali wishes, and mostly everyone sticks to the tried and tested sweets or imported chocolates and cookies. Most of them get passed forward. After all, how many rosogullas or laddoos can one eat? Well, why not delight your friends with some home-made happiness this Diwali, Christmas or Eid?

Here are a few delicious recipes that are also easy to make.

Almond Delight

Soak 1.5 cups of almonds for 4–5 hours in a cup of warm water. Once they have softened, remove their skins and grind them to a paste. To this, add 2 cups of milk and 500 gm sugar and cook in a pan on medium heat. Stir constantly till the sugar melts and the mixture comes to a boil. Add 4 tbsp ghee and cook till the mixture starts leaving the sides of the pan. Sprinkle 1 tsp cardamom powder into it. Pour the mixture onto a greased plate and flatten it out with the help of a spoon or knife. Cool, cut into strips and serve.

Walnut Love

Mix 8 halves of crushed walnuts and 4 deseeded, chopped dates into 1 cup of beaten yoghurt. Drizzle 1 tbsp pure maple syrup on top. Chill, pack in gifting jars and send out.

Cinnamon Sugar

Put castor sugar in a gifting jar with 5–7 large cinnamon sticks. Let this sit for 4 weeks. Your cinnamon sugar is ready to be gifted!

Chakli

Cook and grind ½ cup of moong dal to a thick paste-like consistency. In a big bowl, mix 2 cups of rice flour, the moong dal paste, ½ tsp turmeric, 1 tsp chilli powder, ½ tsp ajwain or cumin seeds and salt to taste. Heat 1 tbsp oil and add it to the rice flour mix. Add water as needed to make a stiff dough. Knead thoroughly by hand, not in a food processor.

Take a lemon-sized ball of the dough and place it in a chakli mould or icing bag with star nozzle. In a thick-bottomed pan, heat oil for frying. Test the oil by dropping a small piece of the dough into it and wait for 3 seconds. If it does not rise to the top, the oil needs to be heated more. Once the oil is hot enough, gently make a spiral with the chakli mould or icing bag and deep-fry the chakli until it is golden brown.

Cool completely before storing in an airtight container.

FIFTY FOUR

Healthy and Delicious Festive Sweets

Food is a big part of any celebration or festival. After all, what's a festival without some goodies? Try making these time-tested and absolutely delicious sweets at home this festive season. Trust me, anything you make at home, even if it is loaded with sugar, is bound to be healthier than something you would pick up from a sweets shop. Besides, home-made sweets always taste the best.

Bengali Chena Poda

Grease an 8-inch round or square ovenproof baking pan or dish. Knead 1 cup of soft cottage cheese with 1 tbsp suji, ¼ cup sugar, 1 tbsp milk, 1 tsp ghee, a few raisins, a few chopped cashews and a pinch of ground cardamom until it is very soft.

Place the mixture into a greased baking pan and bake in a preheated oven at 200 °C for about 45 minutes until the top turns light brown. Let it cool, cut into squares and dig in!

Seedy Bites

Sauté 50 gm muskmelon seeds in 2 tbsp ghee till they turn golden, add 50 gm jaggery and stir continuously for a few minutes until the seeds are sticking to one another. Let the mixture cool down and shape into small, uneven balls.

Milk Cake

Cook 1 l milk, 2 tsp suji and 2 cups of sugar in a kadai, stirring continuously until the mixture thickens. Add ½ cup of ghee and stir it till it becomes non-sticky. Pour this out on a large plate, let it cool. Cut into diamonds and serve.

Besan Barfi

Cook 1 cup besan, ½ cup ghee, 1 cup milk and ½ cup of sugar in a deep pot. Keep stirring constantly over medium heat so that no lumps form till the mixture begins to leave the sides of the pot. Then, add a pinch of cardamom powder, finely sliced nuts (almonds, cashews or pistachios) and seeds (watermelon, pumpkin or sunflower) (optional). Transfer the mixture on a thali or a shallow pan that has been greased with ghee. Once cooled, cut into squares and serve.

Phirni

Bring 1 l milk to a boil in a heavy-bottomed pot and simmer on low heat. Meanwhile, grind 4 tbsp rice (soaked) with just enough water to make a smooth paste. Add a little bit of hot milk to it and mix the rest of it in the hot milk. Continue to cook for 15 minutes till the milk thickens and a smooth mixture forms. Stir in ½ cup of sugar (adjust according to taste). Once the sugar dissolves, remove from heat, pour into serving bowls and set in the fridge. Garnish with sliced nuts and serve chilled.

Cashew Burfi

Bring 250 gm sugar and 250 gm water to a boil, then simmer the mixture on medium heat till the sugar dissolves and the syrup reaches the ideal consistency (to test this, take a drop of the syrup between your thumb and index finger. As you part your fingers, the syrup should form a thread that doesn't break immediately). Stir 500 gm cashew powder into the syrup till the moisture is completely absorbed and the mixture resembles a pliable dough. Transfer to a greased tray and roll or pat it out into a ⅓ inch-thick sheet. Sprinkle chopped pistachios on top. Once it has cooled, cut it with a sharp knife into diamonds and serve.

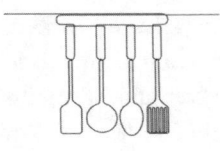

Acknowledgements

I want to thank a lot of people. However, I will begin by thanking all the editors I have worked with across different media houses over the years. I am indebted to each of them for everything they have taught me over the years. I was such a novice when I began writing—my editors shaped my writing and helped me get better with each successive stint. Some of them are such dear, dear friends today, and I love them all.

I am grateful to the entire team at Rupa—my editor Yamini for her support and advice, Saswati and Sneha for editing the book so brilliantly, and, of course, my publisher Kapish for continuing to have faith in my ideas.

Thanks to my agent Anuj Bahri from Redink for relentlessly championing my writing and showcasing my books so brilliantly.

I also wish to thank everyone who has shared their food anecdotes and recipes with me; their stories have made the book so much richer and more meaningful. I extend my gratitude to Charu Sharma, Neeraj Chopra, Ayaan Ali Bangash, Romi Dev, Chitra Narayanan, Chef Tarun Sibal, Bhavana Reddy, Subha J. Rao, Stutee Ghosh, Kiran Manral, Ashok Parija, Kishi Arora, Chef Nishant Choubey, Chef Sabyasachi Gorai and Madhumita Pyne.

Thanks to Chef Manish Mehrotra for writing such a lovely foreword and sharing his recipes and anecdotes with me.

To all my friends who love and encourage me selflessly, I love you.

To my husband Bhanu and my son Vimanyu, thank you for being my world.

My heartfelt gratitude to my sister Punita and her family, especially my darling niece Aarna, for just being there for me all the time.

And, of course, as always, thanks to my parents, whom I love and respect immensely.